"I urge you to get out there in your world. Take responsibility for life. Take action. Have real experiences. Make a lasting difference to at least one person. Create change. Kill the dragon."

— from *Discovery Road* by Andy Brown and Tim Garratt (published by Travellerseye, ISBN 09530575). This book tells of the first successful expedition to ride mountain bikes without support across three continents and, in doing so, raise money for Intermediate Technology. This charity helps poor communities to develop and use skills and technologies which give them more control over their lives, and which contributes to sustainable development. For more information visit their Web site at www.itdg.org.pe

The adjective 'sustainable' provides a link to the charity Sustrans (standing for Sustainable Transport, see www.sustrans.co.uk) whose excellent National Cycle Network runs through East Anglia and is both used by, and links, many of the rides in this book.

Cycling past East Anglian churches?

Many of the routes in this book pass beautiful churches, some more than a thousand years old.
St Nicholas Bracon Ash dates from the 14th century, and is a Grade 1 listed building. £25,000 is needed to stop it falling into disrepair. 5p from the sale of each copy of this book will be donated to the Church Restoration Fund.

St Nicholas Bracon Ash

CYCLE
EAST ANGLIA!

Bob Shingleton

Published by Sigma Leisure – an imprint of
Sigma Press, 1 South Oak Lane, Wilmslow, Cheshire SK9 6AR, England.

British Library Cataloguing in Publication Data
A CIP record for this book is available from the British Library.

ISBN: 1-85058-651-9

Typesetting and Design by: Sigma Press, Wilmslow, Cheshire.

Cover photograph: the author – Route 15
Maps and photographs: the author

Printed by: MFP Design and Print

Disclaimer: the information in this book is given in good faith and is believed to be correct at the time of publication. No responsibility is accepted by either the author or publisher for errors or omissions, or for any loss or injury howsoever caused. Only you can judge your own fitness, competence and experience.

Contents

Routes	Miles	Difficulty	Uses National Cycle Network?
Norwich/S. Norfolk/ Breckland			
1. Norwich & Tas Valley	32 (29)	4+	Yes
2. Wymondham & Old Buckenham	38	3	
3. Thetford Forest	Various	2 to 4	
Broadlands			
4. Foulsham to Reepham	15	2	Yes
5. Reepham & The Marriott's Way	15	1 to 2	Yes
6. Ringland & Taverham	11	3	Yes
7. Blofield & Strumpshaw	7	1	
8. Around Reedham	10	1	
North Norfolk			
9. Castle Acre & Litcham	21	3	
10. Little Walsingham to Burnham Thorpe	21	3	Yes
North Suffolk			
11. Godrick Way	24	3	Yes
12. Peasenhall to Wissett	19	3	Yes
13. Framlingham to Blaxhall	31	3	Yes
Cambridge & beyond			
14. Rutland Water	25 (17)	2 to 3	
15. Ely to Ten Mile Bank	36	4	
16. Grafham Water	10	2	
17. Fotheringay to Bulwick	23	2	
South Suffolk & Essex			
18. Lavenham & East of Sudbury	23	2	
19. Clare & West of Sudbury	21	3	
20. Dedham & The Stour Valley	29	3	Yes
21. Newmarket Cycleway	34	3 to 4	

The Routes

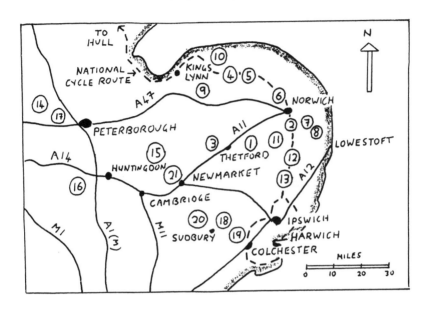

East Anglia: Made for Cycling!

Cycling suits East Anglia; its quiet by-ways, timeless landscape, flat terrain and moderate climate favour the two-wheeled traveller, and "Cycle East Anglia" is written as a guide to help the reader discover the pleasures of this delightful region.

During the writing of this book, I was told by an influential figure in travel publishing, that the new wave was "micro tourism", with travellers covering 20 miles a day by bike instead of 2000 by Concorde. "Cycle East Anglia!" was conceived before I had ever heard of "micro tourism", and it was written simply because there seemed to be a gap in the market for a cycling guide, which not only wrote about the shape of the landscape as seen by a cyclist, but also tried to convey something of its character.

My choice of routes ranging from 7 to 38 miles admirably suits the micro tourist. This is not a book for die-hard hundred-mile-a-day riders. Instead, it aims to appeal to the recreational rider seeking an occasional alternative to the "infernal combustion engine". The use of the Hull to Harwich National Cycle Route as a backbone linking many of the rides, enables more ambitious riders to devise more demanding itineraries of-

Long Staith at Loddon: Route 1

fering up to 280 miles of uninterrupted cycling on quiet or traffic-free roads.

Rather than glossy maps, and colour photos, I have tried to create a resource book for cyclists in the region with 21 routes at the centre. So, as well as routes through popular areas such as The Norfolk Broads you will find notes on everything from Sustrans' admirable National Cycle Network to Chris Boardman's Olympic Gold Medal winning bike which was designed and built in Norfolk.

I am aware that you, the reader, do not spend all your time on your bike, so I have tried to make the book both stimulating to dip into on a wet January evening and useful on the road in August. I have also tried to present a wide variety of rides varying from 7 to 38 miles in length, and offering something for all levels of riders varying from families to experienced tourers.

Thanks at this point are due to those who co-operated in the production of this book and in particular Sigma Press and Graham Beech for backing it. Additional thanks go to Christopher Bishop for his invaluable advice.

Where to Cycle

Although rides are included both around The Broads and the popular north Norfolk coast, these areas do not represent the best cycling in the region. Access to many of the best-known north Norfolk coastal villages such as Blakeney and Brancaster Staithe means using the busy and narrow A149, not recommended for any other than the most intrepid cyclists. While excellent rides are included around Reedham and Blofield (Routes 7 and 8), the nature of many of the Broads means that tow paths and similar cycle ways do not exist, and bike access is therefore restricted. In addition, centres such as Wroxham are very busy in the season, and often overloaded with heavy traffic.These areas are best explored out of the tourist season but a good traffic sense is required at any time on roads such as the A149 and A1151.

East Anglia's best cycling is found in the lesser-known areas, on the Norfolk and Suffolk borders (Routes 11, 12 and 13) and away from the Broads at Reepham (Routes 4 and 5). The areas west of Peterborough are often only seen from cars as visitors hurry to the honeypots of the Broads, but Route 17 from Fotheringay to Bulwick is one of the most memorable in the book.

The Swan at Lavenham: Route 18

The Cycling Agenda

This book started with the words "Cycling suits East Anglia" and the statement is clearly supported by the level of cycling in the region. The 1991 census shows that 9.5 per cent of journeys to work are made by bike in Norwich, more than three times the national average.

In areas such as King's Lynn, where a cycling network has been developed, 14 per cent of journeys to work use bikes, while Kesgrave High School, Ipswich, which is the centre of a local cycling network has the highest proportion of pupils cycling to school anywhere in Britain.

Ipswich BMX track in Landseer Park has the distinction of being the oldest BMX Club in the country, and at the millennium will have been organising cycle racing at club and national levels for twenty years.

These statistics clearly show that a favourable climate and geography, and investment in the correct facilities dramatically increase journeys by bike, and this applies equally to commuter and leisure cycling.

Sustrans

Sustrans stands for 'sustainable transport', and is a charitable organisation working through practical projects such as the National Cycle Net-

Final Approach at Norwich Flyers BMX track

work and Safe Routes to Schools to design and build routes for cyclists and walkers. Details and membership of Sustrans are available from Sustrans, PO Box 21, Bristol BS77 2HA3 – phone 0117 920 0888.

If there are individual jewels of rides in the book, the string holding them together is Sustrans' splendid National Cycle Network Route. Sustrans' vision is a National Cycle Network formed from traffic-free paths on disused railways, towpaths and tracks and on traffic-calmed and minor roads.

A 163-mile section of the National Cycle Network Route runs through East Anglia from the Norfolk port of King's Lynn to Harwich in Essex, passing through Norwich, Great Yarmouth, Lowestoft and Ipswich *en route*. This book has leaned heavily on the National Cycle Network simply because it is so good. Nine of the twenty-one routes use the National Cycle Network for part of their distance, and seven more are within comfortable riding distance. Using this book with the two excellent Sustrans route maps, it is possible to link the nine National Cycle Network Route rides together, to give 280 miles of cycling on quiet or traffic-free roads – enough for a good two weeks of leisure touring.

The Sustrans National Cycle Network is being developed in partnership with over 400 local authorities, and those in East Anglia are showing considerable enterprise in the development of cycling amenities. As an example, Norfolk County Council has an active programme for the encouragement of cycling, including the establishment of cycling forums, involvement with cyclist representative groups and support for the National Cycle Network. Norfolk and other county councils are important supporters of the "England's Cycling Country" project aimed at making East Anglia a key cycling destination. One of the results of this project has been the establishment of several waymarked recreational routes.

Cycle Development in East Anglia

Contributions to the development of cycling in the region have come not just from local government, but also from notable members of the riding community. The flat landscape that hosted so many wartime airfields is ideal cycling country and for competitive cyclists the terrain is perfect for the sport of time trialling.

In the early 1980s, Norfolk-based cyclist and engineer Mike Burrows was attempting to build a superior time-trial bike using aerodynamics as the main lever to achieve better performance. In 1984, Burrows' first "Windcheetah" bike was created using the engineering skills of his pattern-maker father to build a revolutionary carbon-fibre monocoque bike that dispensed with the conventional steel frame.

Despite success in local time trials and interest from the British Cycling Federation, Mike Burrows' innovative bike seemed likely to fall victim to a combination of restrictive regulations from the UCI, the sports ruling body, and a lack of commercial support.

In 1991, however, the outlook started to change for Burrows' radical bike. First, the UCI rules were amended to make the bike race-legal, and then the Norfolk-based car manufacturer Lotus brought much-needed commercial support to the project.

Lotus

A derelict USAF bomber base offered for sale by the Government at Hethel, near Wymondham, was the site chosen by engineer and entrepreneur Colin Chapman when his new Lotus car company outgrew its north London factory in 1966. The years following relocation to Norfolk were the pinnacle of Lotus' achievements with Jim Clark winning both the Formula One World Championship and the Indianapolis 500 race at the wheel of a Lotus. (Ketteringham Hall on Route 2 had the distinction of being both the wartime strategic HQ for the USAAF and home to Chapman's all-conquering Team Lotus.) However, by 1991 both Chapman and Clark were dead, the De Lorean financial scandal with its links to Lotus had rocked the UK financial sector, and Lotus had lurched through several difficult financial periods and owners.

Tantalisingly, at the time of his death, Chapman seemed to be tiring of the technical self-indulgence of Formula One racing, and was looking for new challenges for his engineering genius and minimalist solutions.

On the day he died, in December 1982, a prototype micro-light aircraft was waiting to be flown by him from a purpose-built airstrip at his home in East Carleton (close to Route 2). Chapman's vision was to produce a totally enclosed two-seater, super-light aircraft using the latest composite construction techniques that could be flown without a full pilot's licence.

Following Chapman's death, the micro-light, and several other non-car projects were abandoned so that the beleaguered company could concentrate on financial survival. Chapman would surely have approved of the revolutionary, minimalist composite bike conceived by Burrows and adopted by the Lotus Company.

Fortunately, despite these turbulent times the Hethel-based company had retained a passion both for innovation and competition, encapsulated in its credo of "engineering excellence through competition". Lotus racing driver Rudi Thomann was a member of the same cycling club as Mike Burrows, and in 1991 he showed the innovative "Windcheetah" to Lotus engineers and management. Their senior management realised that the bike contained the core Lotus values of innovation and competition, and saw the double opportunity of pursuing a worthwhile engineering project that could potentially deliver major commercial exposure.

With the backing of senior management, Burrows passed the design rights for the bike to Lotus and an intensive programme of development work started with the 1992 Barcelona Olympics as the goal. The involvement of Lotus gave access to wind tunnel testing and this identified benefits from a radically changed riding position that delivered a major performance improvement.

The rest of the story is history. The combination of Chris Boardman's athletic prowess, Mike Burrows' radical design solution, and Lotus' commercial and engineering input brought triumph in the 4000 metre individual pursuit in Barcelona, and an Olympic Gold Medal to England.

It would be nice to report a sequel to the story with Lotus and Burrows combining to sweep the market with a production version of the bike. However, Lotus' fickle track record of never quite turning brilliant engineering concepts into commercial sucess continued with their excursion into bikes. Further ownership changes and switches in commercial strategy meant that today Lotus' cycling programme is represented solely by Boardman's medal-winning bike as a permanent exhibit in London's Science Museum.

However, Burrows' radical design concept continues to influence performance bike design. Chris Boardman broke the world hour record at Manchester in 1996 riding a Solusport bike designed by Lotus, "inspired" by the 1992 Olympic-winning machine (quotation marks supplied by Mike Burrows when checking this section) and puzzlingly made in South Africa. Burrows has stayed true to his Norfolk roots and runs an engineering company (Burrows Engineering Limited – 01603 721700) at Rackheath outside Norwich, which continues his interest in recumbent and other radical bike design solutions.

The main recognition for Burrows' ground breaking design approach has come sadly not from East Anglia, or even the UK, but from the massive Taiwanese bike conglomerate Giant. They employ him as design consultant on a range of signature bike components, and on a derivative of his "Windcheetah" monocoque design that finally progressed the concept, born as a one-off in 1984, to mass market reality. Burrows' exceptional design skills are also being utilised by Giant on radical commuter bikes that may, hopefully, one day, be seen on the streets of Burrows' native Norwich and other UK cities.

About East Anglia

There is no doubt that cycling is the ideal way to really get the feel for a region, and find what is described in the title of a collection of Lawrence Durell's travel writing as the "Spirit of Place" (ISBN 1569247226).

It was all summed up very well in an article by Rob Story in the excellent US Magazine "Bike".... "On your bike, the land unrolls beneath you at a perfect pace, one tire revolution at a time. Automobiles move too fast to really see the country and walking goes too slow to cover sufficient ground. But bikes are like the microfiche machines in the library, where you can go ploddingly slow or dizzyingly fast and see everything you need to see." (Reprinted with permission from Bike Magazine.)

To help understand the land as it unrolls it is useful to know something about the forces that have shaped it, the geography, history and culture that together define the "Spirit of Place". To this end, the following brief sections are included to help the casual reader understand East Anglia better. Anyone seeking more detailed or scholarly information should turn to the many excellent books on the Region, in particular the Companion Guide to East Anglia (ISBN 1900639026) is recommended. Quotations from this book are by permission of Boydell and Brewer Limited.

Of course, if you already know East Anglia and want to get on with the rides, just flip to the next section!

Where is East Anglia?

For the purposes of this book, East Anglia has been defined as Norfolk, Suffolk, Cambridgeshire and Essex. (Rutland Water just over the boundary in Leicestershire and a ride around Fotheringay in Northamptonshire squeeze in simply because they offer such outstanding cycling.)

Geography and Climate

"Flat and with a lot of water" is the common perception of the geography of East Anglia, and a glance at a relief map of the region shows that there are indeed areas on the Norfolk/Cambridge border which are below sea level.

However, the same map shows the Gog Magog Hills along the southern border of Cambridgeshire reaching the same heights as their easterly neighbours, the Chilterns, while the gently rolling chalk hills of the Norfolk Edge in the north of the county belie its reputation as billiard table flat.

The Broads at Loddon: Route 1

The main relief feature is a chalk ridge, often covered by boulder clay left by retreating glaciers, forming higher ground running south-east/north-west diagonally across the centre of the region. This ridge extends from the Chiltern Hills through the Gog Magog Hills which rise to 220ft (66 m), then through the gently rolling terrain of Suffolk to the Norfolk Edge which reaches the sea to form some dramatic cliffs between Sheringham and Cromer.

The diagonal of chalky uplands leaves areas of lowland on either side. On the south-east seaward side a coastal plain broadens northwards to the wide area of the Norfolk Broads before meeting the chalky hills outside Cromer, while in the west the Fens stretch north from Cambridge to meet the Wash west of King's Lynn.

The Norfolk Broads are the best-known area of East Anglia and attract two million visitors a year. Not only are the Broads a major tourist attraction, but they are also Britain's finest wetland, providing a habitat for a wide variety of wildlife. The Broads are the low-lying, often marshy area between the River Bure in the north and the Waveney in the south, with the River Yare flowing through the middle from Norwich to Great Yarmouth.

These large expanses of water are not a natural feature, but are flooded peat excavations connected to the surrounding villages by channels used in medieval times to transport the fuel. The network of waterways became important commercially with a variety of cargoes being carried on specially built shallow-draught local boats called wherries. In the mid-18th century commercial traffic declined, and was replaced by pleasure cruises, as the building of railways opened the region up to the growing Victorian urban population of the London region.

The geography of East Anglia makes it an ideal habitat for wild life, and birds in particular. The coast is the first land reached by migrating birds, and the dunes, marshes, mud flats and sandbanks are rich in interest for ornithologists. Winter brings huge flocks of waders and winter sea duck. When these depart in the summer, ringed plovers, terns and oystercatchers breed. The coast offers exceptional bird watching, from the winter flocks of waders on the Norfolk side of the Wash to avocets breeding on Orford Ness in Suffolk, and wildfowl and waders on the estuaries of Essex.

The manageable geography of East Anglia combines with an agreeable climate to favour the cyclist. The predominately westerly weather patterns in the UK tend to dump their rainfall on the higher western hills, leaving East Anglia with a moderate and drier climate. The impact in the region of a changing climate and receding water table is well illustrated in the village of Moulton on Route 21. Here, a magnificent four-arch, 15th-century packhorse bridge spans a tiny brook, which is almost invisible at most times of the year.

In recent years rainfall has declined to produce a recurring drought problem, and the annual rainfall for the region is now comparable to more favoured southern holiday destinations, making the region an ideal destination for the touring cyclist.

History and Culture

East Anglia was settled by the Angles early in the 6th century AD, and subsequently ruled by a succession of wealthy Anglo Saxon kings. One of these kings is believed to have been buried, with his fortune of gold and silver, in the famous Sutton Hoo ship, which was excavated near Woodbridge in Suffolk in 1939. (Just off Route 13, Framlingham to Blaxhall.)

From the 7th century there was intermittent conflict in the region sparked off by competition between Roman and Celtic missionaries attempting to convert the inhabitants to Christianity.

The ruins at Castle Acre Priory: Route 9

Two centuries later, raids by Vikings became a serious threat culminating in a major invasion by Danish forces in the autumn of 865, which resulted in East Anglia coming under the control of foreign forces. It was not until 930 that the region was re-conquered by King Alfred's son, Edward The Elder, and East Anglia finally became part of a United Kingdom of England.

Relative prosperity came in the Middle Ages, fuelled by an economy based on wool and proximity to valuable markets such as the Low Countries. This prosperity fuelled a huge increase in population that made the region one of the most densely populated in the British Isles. With this came a programme of building that left a unique legacy of ecclesiastical buildings from modest Saxon churches through the Norman splendour of Norwich Cathedral to the glories of King's College Chapel in Cambridge. It was also during the first part of this period that widespread peat diggings were created in the east of the area. These man-made excavations eventually became flooded to create the network of waterways that today forms the Norfolk Broads (see Routes 1, 7 and 8).

This long period of economic plenty ended in the 19th and early 20th centuries. The double blows of increased competition in the woollen markets from overseas countries, made accessible by the development of steam ships, and the blighting of large tracts of land by serious overgrazing of sheep left the region an economic backwater, despite its proximity to the prosperous London conurbation.

Modern Times

By the start of the 20th century, large areas such as the Brecklands had been reduced to unproductive scrub, and the main activity of parts of the region was raising game to be used as targets by wealthy landowners. The rise of a small but all-powerful group of extremely rich landowners started in the early eighteenth century, and continued through to the building of Sandringham House by Edward, Prince of Wales in 1870.

The activities of these immensely powerful gentry included: the building, in 1762, by the 1st Earl of Leicester of Holkham Hall (see Route 10, Little Walsingham to Burnham Thorpe) – a superlative example of Palladian architecture; and the construction of Houghton Hall (north of Route 9, Castle Acre & Lithcham) by England's first Prime Minister, Sir Robert Walpole. The impact of these wealthy landowners can be judged by the fact that Sir Robert felt that the village of Houghton spoilt the view from his new mansion so he had the houses pulled down and rebuilt where they were out of his sight.

The sad legacy of economic decline and uncaring landlords was a region unequipped to deal with the economic and cultural roller-coaster of the 20th century. Against this background, two outside forces arrived early in the century to re-shape again large parts of the region's landscape. First many of the barren Breckland areas were replanted as forest, including Thetford Forest (see Route 3) which is today the largest lowland pine forest in the country.

Secondly came the more malevolent forces of war, which resulted in 109 air bases being built in the region, and more than 100 000 acres of Norfolk farmland being converted into USAAF bases. A portion of this land never returned to farming but instead is now being used for purposes as diverse as motor racing (Snetterton) and double-glazing manufacture (Horsham St Faith).

Some parts of the region have prospered in the second half of the 20th century. Bury St Edmunds and the south west have flourished in their role as well-to-do commuter areas for London, while Cambridge and its environs have become a centre for high-tech companies resulting in the "silicon fen" label.

Other areas have been less fortunate however. The decline in traditional marine activities such as fishing and sea freight has hit towns including King's Lynn, Great Yarmouth and Lowestoft, creating areas of economic depression that are at considerable odds to the general image of prosperity in the region.

Infrastructure and Industry

Transport has been a major influence on the development of the region, or lack of development, as typified by an important "B" road crossing an "on demand" ferry link less than 80 miles from the M25 (Reedham Ferry on Route 8). Much of the timelessness of the region has been attributed to the poor single carriageway sections of the strategically important A12 and A11.

Admittedly the A14 has been vastly improved and is now fully dual carriageway as it cuts through the region to Felixstowe, excellent for container lorry drivers but of limited use for visitors to Norfolk. Both this county and Suffolk incidentally have the distinctive attribute of possessing not one single mile of motorway between them as they enter the 21st century. To a certain extent, the historic isolationism of East Anglia as underlined by conquering Viking and Danish forces has now shifted to a marginalisation caused by a poor trunk road network. This isolation is largely responsible for the appeal of the region, and explains how it can be so different from not-so-distant London.

The Economy

Despite its visual dominance, agriculture is a declining and increasingly minor employer in East Anglia. Cereals, sugar beet, pigs and poultry are the most important products, but increasing mechanisation and intensive farming of large holdings means that agriculture is no longer the area's dominant employer.

As with so much of the UK, the ubiquitous service sector now dominates the employment market with almost 50 per cent of the workforce employed in areas as diverse as Financial Services (Norwich Union and Virgin Direct) to telecommunications (BT). This figure is ten times larger than the agricultural labour force, although ancillary services such as food processing and distribution considerably boost the total size of the workforce linked to farming.

East Anglia is still a unique and relatively isolated region, but images of it as a rural economy are simply an illusion. Increasingly the outlying villages are providing homes for workers in the new service economies of Norfolk, Ipswich and Cambridge.

The isolation of the more remote fringes of Norfolk coupled with the individual nature of the local people bears comparison with parts of Scotland. It is probably no coincidence that late in the last century, kilted highlanders drove cattle from Scotland to the meadows around Reedham (Route 8) for fattening before selling them in Norwich Market. I was reminded of this when out researching Route 2 on a typically cold, windy Norfolk afternoon. As I cycled near Flordon, I heard a strange wailing which I took to be the wind in the nearby power cables. I was rather surprised to ride further on and find a lone bagpiper practicing far from his neighbours by the roadside.

East Anglian Characters

East Anglia's unique geography has resulted in both a landscape and people with strongly individual characteristics. Norfolk saw one of the few (temporarily) successful attempts in England to resist illegal land enclosures and depopulation in 1549. Robert Kett, who was eventually defeated and hung from the parapets of Norwich Castle, (Route 1) led the resistance starting from Wymondham (pronounced "Windum") – see Route 2.

Norfolk nurse, Edith Cavell (born in Mulbarton – see Route 2) also summed up this individualism. Serving as a matron of a clinic in occupied Belgium in 1915 she was arrested by the Germans for helping allied servicemen to escape to Holland and was shot by order of the German High Command. Lord Nelson is arguably East Anglia's most famous son; the great sea commander was born near the water's edge in the North Norfolk village of Burnham Thorpe (Route 10).

Individual voices from East Anglia can also be heard in the worlds of music and literature. The East Anglian coast inspired Benjamin Britten who was born in Lowestoft and founded the Aldeburgh Festival (at Snape, off Route 13), while E. J. Moeran wrote several works heavily influenced by the region (a budget-priced recording of his chamber works on Naxos 8554079 is highly recommended). One of Britain's greatest (and most under-rated) living composers today lives in Attleborough (off Route 2), near Norwich. Sir Malcolm Arnold is the composer of nine magnificent, and little known, symphonies. His English and Scottish dances are better known, but he will surely be remembered as a prolific film composer whose credits include *The Bridge Over The River Kwai*.

The solitude and beauty of East Anglia has made it both the inspiration and home for many writers. Rupert Brooke immortalised a village outside Cambridge in his poem "The Old Vicarage, Grantchester", although this Rectory today has more mundane literary connections as the home of politician and sometime novelist Geoffrey Archer. Today, writers living in the region range from Malcolm Bradbury through Elizabeth Jane Howard to Delia Smith (who is also linked to the region, at the time of writing, through majority ownership of the perennially underperforming Norwich City Football Club).

The unique qualities of sky, light and atmosphere provided the catalyst for the careers of several great painters, notably John Constable who immortalised the village of East Bergholt and the Stour Valley (Routes 18, 19 & 20.) in paintings such as "The Haywain".

These diverse threads – ancient churches, great houses, unique landscapes and strong individuals – combine to offer a heady mixture that will absorb and inspire any visitor. Getting to know the region using a bike is not just convenient, it also compliments a culture that has always had to work with, rather than against, the landscape. Cycling is still thankfully today an appropriately individual and self-sufficient form of transport that compliments the attractions of East Anglia.

Churches

East Anglia has so much to offer visiting cyclists. One of its great treasures is its churches. Examples such as St Peter and St Paul at Salle (off Routes 4 and 5) will surely strike cords in even the most hardened agnostic. From a practical point of view churches and pubs remain the sole manmade landmarks in a landscape which has seen many other features disappear with progressive depopulation since the Middle Ages.

It is remarkable that many of the finest churches are more than one thousand years old. Is it not worth marvelling at them in contrast to our own secular and vacuous architectural marking of the Millennium? I wonder who will be writing a book of bike rides in a thousand years' time visiting the Greenwich Dome, or will that empty bauble long since have crumbled into oblivion while the simple Saxon Towers of East Anglia remain as reminders of a less material age?

Nowhere else in the British Isles can so many fine churches be seen in such a compact area, with some examples dating back more than 1000 years. East Anglia's architectural wealth is all the more impressive considering that other than flint there is no local stone in the area. The scarcity of local building materials is illustrated by the fact that St Peter's Hall, visited on Route 11, used stones that originated from Caen in Normandy.

The region has its grand sacred buildings, notably Ely (Route 15) and Norwich (Route 1) cathedrals. No less remarkable are the hundreds of parish churches that are spread north from the once wealthy west Suffolk towns of Lavenham (Route 18) and Bury St Edmunds into Norfolk and west to the Fens.

Norfolk has the most remarkable wealth of parish churches and their frequency on the ground is a reflection of the fact that in medieval times this region was both wealthy and heavily populated. It may be difficult for today's cyclist travelling through the open and desolate Norfolk landscape to accept that this was once one of Britain's most densely populated reions, but even toay the population of Norfolk is greater than apparently more populous (but smaller) counties such as Berkshire and Oxfordshire.

The church at Lavenham: Route 18

The wealth generated by the wool trade fuelled medieval ecclesiastical building in Suffolk, and more particularly in Norfolk, and this has left a legacy ranging from Saxon churches with their distinctive round towers through to the chapel started by Henry VI for King's College, Cambridge. Many of the medieval churches were "improved" or, more accurately, modified in the 19th century, but fortunately the distinctive Saxon and Norman towers remain to act as landmarks in the flat landscape.

Thankfully the majority of the rural parish churches remain in use as places of worship – the area's Methodist and Baptist chapels have not fared so well and many have been converted into dwellings or stand disused (Route 8 passes a typically isolated and deserted Methodist chapel outside Reedham). However, few of the grand rectories house rectors, most have been sold by the church commissioners and are now trophies for successful businessmen. Today's East Anglian Rector typically lives in a modern brick house and has responsibility for three or more scattered churches.

Where possible churches of note have been included on the rides, these range from the modest Saxon gem at Forncett St Peter (Route 2) through to the Norman splendour of Norwich Cathedral, accessible from Norwich city centre (Route 1).

Richard Tilbrook's excellent book "Norfolk Churches" (Jarrold ISBN 0711709610) is highly recommended for its superb photos and enlightening text.

Wartime East Anglia

This section is of more relevance than just background reading in a book on cycling. The geology of the region has made it equally suitable for both flying planes and riding bikes. A tradition of military and agricultural engineering has helped develop a cycling- friendly light engineering culture. As an example, the Lotus car factory (close to Route 2), provided the engineering skills to help produce Mike Burrow's Olympic gold medal winning bike, was built in 1966 on a disused airfield. This was previously being used as a War Department equipment disposal site littered with old military equipment, including broken aeroplanes, lorries and gun carriers. At the same time, the high-tech industries that have grown from wartime electronic projects in the region have created a "silicon fen" based in Cambridge, and soon to host Microsoft's European headquarters. Already Cambridge is considered by many to be the cycling capital of England, and parallels with Palo Alto, Seattle, and similar pro-cycling West Coast cities can only help strengthen the cycling traditions of the area.

It was inevitable that East Anglia would play an important role in the

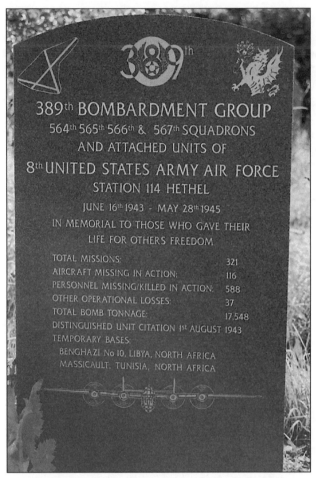

389th BOMBARDMENT GROUP
564th 565th 566th & 567th SQUADRONS
AND ATTACHED UNITS OF
8th UNITED STATES ARMY AIR FORCE
STATION 114 HETHEL
JUNE 16th 1943 - MAY 28th 1945
IN MEMORIAL TO THOSE WHO GAVE THEIR
LIFE FOR OTHERS FREEDOM

TOTAL MISSIONS:	321
AIRCRAFT MISSING IN ACTION:	116
PERSONNEL MISSING/KILLED IN ACTION:	588
OTHER OPERATIONAL LOSSES:	37
TOTAL BOMB TONNAGE:	17,548

DISTINGUISHED UNIT CITATION 1st AUGUST 1943
TEMPORARY BASES:
BENGHAZI No 10, LIBYA, NORTH AFRICA
MASSICAULT, TUNISIA, NORTH AFRICA

8th US Air Force Memorial at Hethel Church:
Route 2

Second World War. As the closest allied territory to the German heartland, and the coast facing the occupied Low Countries, the region was of key strategic importance. When to this was added flat terrain ideally suited to military airbases, it was certain that the war with Germany would have a major and lasting impact on the region.

As well as being in the front line for air and sea attacks, the region was the centre of strategic activities central to the allied war effort. There were 109 airbases in the area hosting squadrons from eight countries. Important and secret technical developments took place in the region. Radar was developed on the Suffolk coast, and there were several weapons-testing ranges that were cloaked in secrecy.

The invasion of Holland in August 1940 meant that only the sea separated East Anglia from the German invasion forces. Dual efforts were made both to increase security in the region and rapidly increase food production as the U-boat stranglehold prevented the import of essential foodstuffs. Huge tracts of East Anglia had been turned over to scrub for raising game birds, and the task of reclaiming these areas for agriculture was Herculean.

East Anglia came under dual attack from both the sea and air. Fast and deadly German E-boats lurked off the coast with one channel between Happisburgh Sands and the Norfolk coast becoming known as "E-boat Alley" with the German predators claiming huge casualties amongst slow moving convoys. Aerial bombing also caused terrible damage, with Norwich in particular being hit many times with the Bolton and Paul engineering works near the city centre being a main target. The site of this factory is today the scene for a massive urban redevelopment programme, with the final route of the National Cycle Route No 1 being part of the scheme (Route 1).

The worst bomb damage was inflicted on Norwich in April 1942 when 158 civilians were killed in one night of what became known as the "Baedeker" raids. The name came from the use of the famous German Baedeker Guide Book by Hitler to select target towns with the greatest architectural and cultural heritage.

The main impact on East Anglia came from the American bases in the region. By 1942, 100 000 acres of Norfolk farmland had been handed over for USAAF bases. This caused a massive change to the landscape with each airfield having three runways, the main one more than a mile long. The longevity of the airbase runways and buildings mean that many survive today. (Route 2 alone passes three such airfields.)

At this distance, it is difficult to appreciate the impact the arrival of the American airforce had on a county like Norfolk. In his excellent book "Norfolk Airfields in the Second World War" (ISBN 1-85306-320-7, published by Countryside Books), Graham Smith describes how in 1939 more than 400 rural Norfolk parishes had no public water supply, large parts of the county still had no mains electricity and telephones were still a novelty. The Norfolk locals with their strong accent and conservative culture contrasted starkly with the visiting Americans who were famously described as "overpaid, oversexed and over here"!

The cultural impact of the Americans is only overshadowed by the contribution and sacrifice that they made towards the Allied victory. The Memorials at Hethel (Route 2), Seething (Route 1) and many other villages are a sobering reminder of the horrendous losses suffered by American, British and other aircrews during Hitler's war.

About the Routes

All 21 routes are circular, and avoid covering the same stretch of road twice wherever possible. I find that rides which require either retracing hard-won miles or, worse still, a *Tour de France* style support car to be an admission of defeat. The **distance** is given for each route. When refreshment breaks and map reading stops are included, the **average speed** on a bike can be surprisingly slow, around 8 to 12 mph for these routes, depending on conditions and experience. A **difficulty level** from 1 (easy) to 4 (difficult) is given to help selection of rides.

The highest priority was placed on planning routes that avoid roads with heavy traffic. Heavy motor traffic is the enemy of the cyclist, who needs quiet roads. Wherever possible, cycling on "A" roads has been avoided altogether, and the use of "B" roads has been minimised. Several routes use traffic-free paths for the majority of the ride, others use shorter off-road sections. One ride (Route 17) covers 23 miles on tarmac without once touching an "A" or "B" road. The focus on relatively traffic-free routes has forced some unfortunate omissions, notably any routes passing through the city of Cambridge. The longest ride in this book, Route 2 (Wymondham to Old Buckenham) does not touch one "A" road — even to cross — in its 38-mile length, while Route 17 (Fotheringay to Bulwick) does not use a single inch of "A" or "B" roads in 23 miles. Planning routes such as these require a fair amount of careful research, hopefully the value added by this work alone will help justify the purchase of this book by delivering enjoyable and quiet cycling.

I assume the traveller has a modicum of technical competence, and (where possible) nearby bike shops are mentioned. I have tried to indicate when a route is likely to require a mountain bike. Apart from this, I have avoided lecturing the reader on choice of bike, clothing or riding style. My first and totally agreeable experience of mountain biking more than a decade ago, was on rough Scottish tracks. I was riding a cheap Raleigh that would never grace the pages of the then-unborn mountain bike press. This experience has left me with a healthy dose of cynicism about trends (or should it be fashions?) in cycling technology.

Routes & Maps

Giving route directions in a book such as this is always difficult, and the draconian Ordnance Survey copyright enforcement means the included maps are of limited value. It is strongly recommended that the relevant Ordnance Survey Landranger Maps be used.

The route is best transferred onto the map using a 6B pencil before the ride. The author used an excellent Ortlieb map holder around his neck displaying the relevant OS sheet for all the rides. The route directions have been written in narrative form rather than the "bullet point" style used in other publications. This is to allow some background commentary on the places and buildings visited to be included. All photographs (taken on a Nikon F50) are copyright of the author.

I can honestly say I rode every inch of the 455 miles of routes covered in the book over six winter and spring months. During those miles I did not suffer one puncture, or get seriously wet! I hope that you find the riding as enjoyable as I found the researching.

Bikes & Cycling

For the technically minded, the following three bikes were used to explore the routes in this book. For the off-road rides a 1990 TREK 990 MTB with rigid forks coped admirably. For on-road a 1988 MS Racing Mountain Bike fitted with semi-slick tyres was my workhorse. A Moulton APB-14 transportable also covered several of the routes, chosen primarily for ease of transport by car, but also because the full suspension and 20-inch wheels make this a singularly individual and practical bike.

Sources

No book can pretend to be a definitive guide to cycling in the region. The choice of routes is subjective, and is best viewed as a sample of the cycling delights on offer. Because of the size of the region, the spread of rides between counties is uneven with an unashamed bias towards Norfolk and Suffolk, both because these are the quintessential East Anglian counties and because of personal knowledge.

Use has been made of several local authority documented routes, plus of course the groundbreaking Sustrans Hull to Harwich Cycle Route. When possible, the sources of previously published routes have been acknowledged and contact addresses given.

There are a number of Web sites giving useful information about East Anglia. Of the Tourist Boards, www.broadland.com is one of the best with helpful links to many other sites. Useful maps and other information including details of accommodation are available on http://uk.multimap.com. The University of East Anglia Cycling Club site at www.uea.ac.uk/~sucycle has some good information including a map of teashops and other refreshment stops.

Although excellent off-road routes are covered, including those in Thetford Forest, Rutland Water and The Marriott's Way, the cycling strength of East Anglia does not really lie in off-road mountain biking. The relatively flat terrain coupled with soft soils and a large equestrian population can work against the hard core mountain biker. Instead, it is the multitude of quiet back roads and lanes that offer most to the cyclist. These represent ideal cycling territory but it is prudent to warn of speeding cars (and agricultural vehicles) and farmers can deposit a lot of slippery material on the tarmac surface.

There is so much to enjoy in this region, from the challenge of Rutland Water in the west, to the panoramic skies and marshes of Broadland in the east. If this book helps to open your eyes to the pleasures of the area it will have done its job admirably and I hope it may prompt you to "Cycle East Anglia".

Hazards of cycling

East Anglia offers compelling cycling, but I must warn the rider of potential hazards on each route. I have not set out to write a promotional leaflet for tourism, but rather a practical guide to cycling the region's roads.

The reader should not be lulled into thinking that East Anglia is cycling nirvana. Trunk roads such as the A14, A11 and A47 are nightmares of lumbering lorries and speeding cars, and present a problem for the cyclist even to cross, let alone ride along. Despite the efforts of local government, Norwich remains a beautiful city held hostage by the motor car, and only dramatic surgery will reverse this balance in favour of less damaging means of transport.

Although all the routes have been ridden and documented by the author, their inclusion is not a guarantee of the legal right to ride, and features on the ground do change. Readers are invited to forward any amendments to the author, care of the publisher. The author, publisher and other parties cannot take responsibility for injury or loss resulting from following these routes, cycling can be dangerous.

The Routes

Route 1
Norwich Yare and Tas Valleys

Distance: 32 miles

Difficulty Level: Full Route: 4+.
Without Norwich City Loop: 3

Map: OS Landranger 134 – Norfolk and The Broads

Setting the Scene

This ride is big in every sense. At 32 miles in length it is one of the biggest in the book. There are big changes in surroundings, from the placid lower reaches of the Yare to the bustle of Norwich City centre. The full route also offers some big cycling challenges, and the central Norwich section should only be attempted by cyclists with considerable experience of urban riding. A short cut is available which cuts out the city centre section to form a route suitable for reasonably experienced leisure cyclists.

The starting point of the ride is Whitlingham Country Park, on the banks of the Yare, to the west of Norwich where there is a large and free car park. The National Cycle Network passes though the park and can be used as a direct route into the centre of Norwich for sight seeing.

The ride follows the Yare downstream from Norwich to Loddon using the National Cycle Network. After Loddon the ride crosses the watershed to join the Tas at Stoke Holy Cross, and then follows this river back into Norwich.

There is something for everyone on this ride. The attractions of Norwich itself could easily fill a book. Out in the country there are pubs too numerous to mention, riverside attractions and the Roman remains at Caistor St Edmund.

With the contrasts of city and remote riverside, this ride offers big challenges and big rewards. It is thoroughly recommended to the experienced cyclist.

What to Expect

An optional shortcut divides the ride into a 29-mile rural ride which scores a difficulty level of three largely due to its length, and a three-mile loop into Norwich city centre which, despite the use of cycle lanes and railway paths, scores an over-maximum four-plus difficulty level.

If the short loop didn't give access to the delights of Norwich City centre it would not be included in this book. There are sections where very busy roads have to be used (including one on the National Cycle Network), and the Norwich ride is recommended only for skilled and experienced riders used to city traffic.

The rural ride includes a short section of rough bridleway on the National Cycle Network which is really only suitable for mountain bikes. However, directions are given to easily by-pass this section so that the ride is suitable for all types of bikes.

The ride is excellently endowed with pubs, perhaps too well, as the first tempting riverside inn is just a few miles from the start. There is a good selection of shops in Loddon, and Norwich has several good bike shops, one of the best being Freewheel (01603 610072) in Prince of Wales Road, which is only a short distance off the route. The workshop at John Borwell Cycles (01603 787736) in Spencer Street enjoys a high local reputation, particularly for wheel building.

Rockland Broad

Getting Started

Starting Point: Whitlingham Country Park – OS Grid Ref. TG 254079.

Reach the car park by leaving the County Hall roundabout on the A147 Norwich outer ring road in the direction signposted to Trowse with the National Cycle Network sign. Cross the railway bridge and turn left opposite Trowse church into Whitlingham Lane, which is signposted to the Ski Club.

Drive along Whitlingham Lane past the dry ski slope on the right. Stay straight ahead over the cattle grid and turn into the large car park on the left. Norwich railway station is only a very short distance off the route.

This ride can easily be linked to others to the north and south using the National Cycle Network as the link. Other Routes including 7 and 8 (Reedham and Blofield) across the Yare, and Route 2 (Wymondham to Old Buckenham) are within easy cycling distance.

The Route

From the exit of the car park turn right back in the direction from which you came in, and ride back out across the cattle grid. After the cattle grid, take the right turn, which drops down to the river. You are now on the National Cycle Network, which heads out east along the Yare, away from Norwich. This ride follows the Sustrans route all the way to the far side of Loddon.

The route passes several gravel pits and rejoins the tarmac road. Go left onto this road in the direction signposted for the National Cycle Network and ride past some new gravel workings. After a short stretch of woodland there is a very pleasant ride along the Yare past more car parking and toilets on the right.

Behind the car park on the right is a small quarry that offers some extreme mountain biking. There are some heart-stopping drop-offs that must be rated "strictly for the most extreme riders with a diminished sense of self-preservation".

The road then turns right away from the river with a ruined church on a knoll on the right, and then passes under the new A47 Southern By-pass. Follow the National Cycle Network signs as the road zigzags up the hill to reach the Anglian Water sewage works at the top. Beware on this section as the concrete road is shared with slurry tankers, the message on these is "non hazardous load", which is more than can be said for some of their

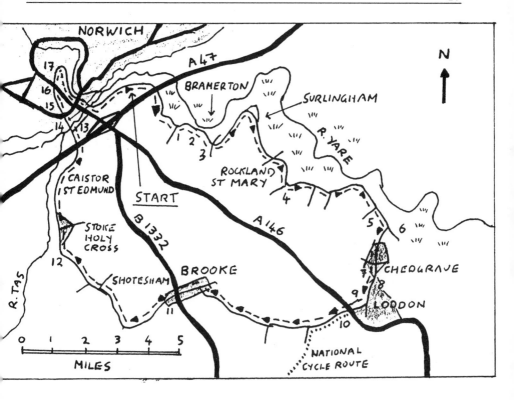

drivers! The driver of the vehicle I met clearly thought that users of the National Cycle Network were there on sufferance.

Stay on this access road as it drops downhill and then climbs to a bridleway on the left (1), which you take through a gate, the track is signposted to Kirby Bedon and has a National Cycle Network sign. (This short but fairly rough and possibly muddy off-road section can be avoided by simply ignoring the bridle path and riding to the end of the access road. Turn left out on to the main road and first left again to bring you back to point (2) on the route.) Keep climbing on the bridleway as the view to your left opens to include the new A47 bridge over the Yare and Carrow Road, the home of Norwich City Football Club. The road drops fairly steeply downhill through a section where the farmer has tried to derail the National Cycle Network by churning it up, before reaching another gate.

At this gate turn left (2) out on to the tarmac road in the direction of the National Cycle Network sign. The lane runs between high hedgerows and drops down to reach the river at the Woods End pub in a marvellous location right on the water's edge. Cycle past the pub (if you can resist the temptation) and the big riverside houses.

The road then leaves the river with a steep (granny ring if you are on a mountain bike) climb. Keep straight ahead in the direction of Bramerton ignoring the left turn until you reach a T-junction. Go left **(3)** at this junction in the direction signposted to Surlingham and marked with a National Cycle Network pointer. This road gains some altitude and the huge sugar beet factory at Cantley starts to come into view on the right.

The road then drops down to Surlingham past Hill Farm on your left and past Surlingham church with its round Norman tower again on your left. Ride away from the church in the direction signposted to Surlingham Ferry and, at the bottom of a gentle downhill, stay on the main road, which now becomes Walnut Hill. Ignoring the turning down to Surlingham Ferry, climb Walnut Hill past the Nurseries to reach the main part of Surlingham with the village pond on the left, with a Post Office and village store.

Keep on the main road through the village following the signposts marked Rockland and Claxton into Mill Road. The road leaves the village and crosses open fields with a 360-degree panorama including the River Yare to your left with the Cantley sugar beet factory clearly visible. The area beyond the factory on the far side of the river is covered in Route 8 (Reedham) which can be reached via Reedham Ferry beyond Loddon. The road drops into Rockland St Mary past a new housing development on the left, before reaching a T-junction in the village.

Turn left **(4)** here signposted to Claxton and Langley and marked with a National Cycle Network flag. The road drops down from Rockland and at the bottom is New Inn which sits at the head of Rockland Broad. This wide Broad connected to the Yare by a narrow channel makes it easier to understand the origins of the Broads as flooded peat workings.

Leaving the New Inn the road continues on into Claxton with a church on the skyline to the right. Ride straight ahead in the direction signposted to Loddon, through the village, and then continue on the main road towards Langley and Loddon ignoring the various turnings on the right.

The ride follows the flood plain of the Yare here. There are few major features, just a marvelous vista of the river with the solitary stump of a windmill, and birds continuously remind you that this is an area rich in wildlife. The Cantley sugar beet factory is now a major feature contrasting sharply with the surrounding natural landscape.

After passing some interesting old farm buildings on the left, Langley

Green is reached. At the War Memorial go straight ahead **(5)** into Langley Street turning off the main road in the direction signposted to Langley Street and Hardley, continuing to follow the National Cycle Network signs. Just after the War Memorial is the Wherry Pub on the right.

A mile after this turning take the right turn **(6)** signposted to Loddon and marked with a National Cycle Network flag up a road called Gentleman's Walk. On the left, a deserted village school is a sad reminder of the more prosperous history of this area. Gentleman's Walk climbs sway from the river; it is worth stopping at the top, by the houses, to look back over the magnificent view of the Yare Valley.

The road crosses fields; go straight ahead at the crossroads in the direction signposted to Loddon and marked with a National Cycle Network flag into Snow Lane. The road now drops down into Chedgrave, and reaches a T-junction with Langley Road where you take the left **(7)** signposted to Loddon with a National Cycle Network flag. Ride straight ahead through the small village of Chedgrave following the signs to Loddon until you reach a T-junction with the White Horse pub opposite.

Turn left **(8)** at this junction into the main road, which brings you to the River Chet at Long Staith. On the right is an old watermill and, on the left, boatyards, a marina and toilets. Long Staith was an active centre for water transport using the distinctive wherries. These unique East Anglian vessels were large, shallow-draft, single-sailed boats used for transporting coal and wheat. There are shops and other amenities in Loddon.

Climbing away from Long Staith take the right turn **(9)** signposted to Seething and Brooke marked with a National Cycle Network flag. Ride out past St John's Chapel on the right and then up past Loddon High School on the left, to meet the busy A148.

Go diagonally across the A148 **(10)** into Mundham Road opposite, which is signposted to Mundham and Sisland, and which is a straight ride through to Brooke almost five miles away. After three-quarters of a mile the National Cycle Network turns left and heads south towards Bungay; ignore this turning and stay heading on the tarmac road west to start the journey back towards Norwich.

The road gains altitude and the two church towers of Nundham and Seething come into view only half a mile apart. St Peter's in Mundham is first passed on the right, and then the Saxon tower of St Margaret and St Remigius in Seething.

The turning alongside the church in Seething leads to the airfield that was used by the USAF 448 Bomber Group in the Second World War and a memorial in the churchyard is a poignant reminder of the 350 American aircrew from Seething killed in action. The Memorial Museum to the American airmen is housed in the renovated control tower at Seething and is open on the first Sunday in each month from May to October.

Leaving behind the church continue on the main road in the direction of Brooke, passing first through the oddly named hamlet of Lingh, and then to Kirstead with the parish church of St Margaret on the left, and the magnificent Kirstead Hall opposite.

The road then reaches Brooke. Stay on the main road as it bears left past the pond in the direction signposted to Poringland and Shotesham to reach the busy B1332. Cross the main road **(11)** into the lane opposite, called High Green, on the right is the Kings Head pub and a shop.

Go straight along High Green past the primary school, village stores and Baptist Chapel on the right, and then out of the village into open farmland with woods and the pretty Keepers Cottage on the right. Stay on the main road in the direction of Shotesham, ignoring the various side turnings, as the road winds between fields and woodland. On the left the valley of a tributary of the River Tas comes into view, you will now follow the Tas all the way back to Norwich.

The road then drops down and enters Shotesham. Cycle through the village and leave it past the church on a hillock on the left, then continue on the main road in the direction signposted to Stoke Holy Cross.

On the outskirts of Shotesham you pass the Globe pub on the right, the road then meanders towards Stoke Holy Cross, along the edge of the Tas valley. This is a remarkably peaceful rolling landscape less than six miles from the centre of Norwich.

The road climbs to a T-junction opposite Stoke Holy Cross parish church, turn right **(12)** here in the direction signposted to Caistor and Norwich. Freewheel into Stoke Holy Cross, with views across the valley to Dunston Hall, now a hotel and leisure centre with tennis courts and mandatory golf course.

Ride straight through Stoke Holy Cross in the direction signposted to Caistor, passing the Wilderbeest Arms with its renowned restaurant on the right. A short distance separates Stoke Holy Cross and Caistor St Edmund where, on the left, are the remains of the Roman town which was once Norfolk's capital. 1700 years ago this area was surrounded by high walls and contained a large bustling market town with a centre of local government, trade and entertainment. Caistor is one of a few Roman towns in Britain that has not been damaged or hidden by later buildings.

There is an excellent guided walk around the ruins, which also contain the church of Caistor St Edmund.

The road drops down passing Caistor Hall on the right then goes straight ahead at the crossroads in the direction signposted to Arminghall. After Caistor the new A47 Southern By-pass can be seen and heard ahead of you, and the road crosses it on a bridge, which gives good views towards Norwich. On the right is the ugly block of County Hall beyond which the ride started.

The road drops down from the bridge, at the bottom of the descent is a right turn **(13)** into White Horse Lane. (This turn should be taken if you want to return to Trowse and the starting point without taking the loop into central Norwich). The main route continues straight ahead ignoring this right turn, and crosses the river and railway on a single bridge to reach the Cock Public House which is pleasantly situated by the river and provides an ideal spot for a break before facing the rigours of the Norwich traffic.

Take the left turn **(14)** opposite the Cock Public House into Mansfield Lane, which climbs to a T-junction. Go right here and continue climbing crossing another railway bridge, which leads to a set of traffic lights at the crossroads with the Outer Ring Road **(15)**.

Go straight ahead at these traffic lights into Mansfield Lane on the other side, and then climb through the housing estate and immediately after Beeching Road on your left take the path on the left. Go left again **(16)** by the Norwich City Council sign and up a small bank onto the Hall Road railway path. Go right on this railway path and head in towards Norwich.

The railway path brings you out at the end of a road, which leads up past a large Sainsbury's store on your right. As the road turns right take the middle cycle lane, which leads you to a cyclists' box at the next traffic lights (do cyclists ever feel safe sitting in these boxes with impatient motorists and lorry drivers inches from their back wheel?).

At the traffic lights **(17)** go straight ahead into All Saints Green and at the next set of traffic lights go straight ahead again to reach Bonds Department Store on your right. Follow the road as it bears left, then pull over into the right-hand lane, and turn right **(18)** at the next set of traffic lights opposite Marks & Spencer into Red Lion Street. Great care is needed on this section of the ride; you are now in the habitat of the urban motorist.

With Norwich Castle dead ahead follow the road round to the left in the direction signposted to Lowestoft, and ride along Castle Meadow in the shadow of the Castle. (At the time of writing Castle Meadow has been closed to cars, but not cycles, taxis and buses for an experimental period.)

At the next set of traffic lights go straight ahead in the direction signposted to Great Yarmouth, while keeping over in the right-hand lane. Cross two sets of traffic lights while keeping to the right, and after the second of Anglia Television buildings turn sharp right **(19)** into King Street, a one way street, which is part of the National Cycle Network.

Cycle along King Street using the bike lane to the next set of traffic lights, and go straight ahead ignoring the dead-end signs — there is cycle access from the other end.

Ride along this pleasant cobbled traffic-free street with the church of St Peter Parmentergate on your right. At the end of this street go through the barrier out on to the one way street following the National Cycle Network signs, and follow King Street to the end passing the Ferry Boat Pub on your left. With its pleasant waterside garden, the Ferry Boat is an excellent place to celebrate the fact that you are now only 1 ¼ miles from the end of the ride.

At the end of King Street go left **(20)** at the T-junction which brings you to the very busy A147 Ring Road. Go straight ahead out onto the main road in the direction signposted as the National Cycle Network. This section of main road can be hideously busy, and at peak times is unsuitable for cyclists despite being part of the temporary National Cycle Network. If in doubt walk the short distance on the pavement to the next set of traffic lights and cycle path.

The skilled cyclist should ride up the short hill to the traffic lights. Go left **(21)** at these lights onto the pavement to join the official cycle path, which drops downhill to the next roundabout opposite County Hall. Go straight ahead **(22)** at this roundabout, remaining on the cycle path, and pick up the signs for the National Cycle Network which are signposted to Poringland and Kirby Bedon.

Just before the railway bridge the cycle path ends, continue on the road over the bridge, then opposite the church turn left **(23)** signposted to Ski Club and National Cycle Network to Whitlingham. Cycle straight ahead along Whitlingham Lane past the dry Ski Slope, over the cattle grid, and turn left into the car park from where the ride started.

Route 2
Wymondham to Old Buckenham

Distance: 38 miles

Difficulty Level: 3

Maps: OS Landranger 144 – Breckland and Wymondham; OS Landranger 134 – Norwich and The Broads

Setting the Scene

There are enough delights and surprises in this 38-mile ride to keep the rider entranced right to the end. The route starts and finishes in the South Norfolk town of Wymondham, which is dominated by the two towers of its Abbey church.

The surprises start as soon as the rider gets close to the Abbey, for it is clear that the two towers at either end of the church are not only totally different, but one is unfinished and the other is part of the ruins of a monastic building that was once twice its current size.

The extraordinary plan of the church is a legacy of its original use by both the Benedictine community and the town people as a parish church. In the 13th century, a dispute arose between the priory and the local people, which finally resulted in Pope Innocent IV ruling on the subdivision of the church. A continuing disagreement between the two factions resulted in the two parts of the church being effectively partitioned, with only the eastern tower of the monastic church still standing.

There are other delightful churches to see on the ride, albeit not on the scale of Wymondham Abbey. Nevertheless, those at Forncett St Peter, Bracon Ash and Hethel are well worth visiting.

There is much else to surprise and delight as well as churches. The route passes Hethel airfield, once an important USAF base and now the high tech home of Lotus Cars.

The villages of Mulbarton and Old Buckenham are amongst several claiming to have the largest village green in Norfolk. New Buckenham itself is an interesting example of early town planning with the plan set out in the 15th century around the castle.

Some of the surprising diversity of this area of South Norfolk is derived from its geology. The heavy clay is too wet for sheep farming, and this meant that the agricultural land was not combined into large estates by unscrupulous landowners in the 16th century. Due to this, the trend of prairie-sized sheep farms with their massive open fields that dominate huge areas of North Norfolk has been avoided, leaving more modest farms, smallholdings and other enterprises to add variety to the landscape. The ride passes a world renowned car factory, a large poultry farm and two active airfields as well as many small farms on its route.

Many visitors only see South Norfolk as they hurtle up the A11 in their cars on the last leg of the journey to Norwich and The Broads. The small detour off the A11 into Wymondham to start this extremely pleasant and not unduly taxing ride is highly recommended as a way of exploring a quiet and less-known area of East Anglia which is all the more remarkable for being so close to Norwich. This ride is one of the author's favourites, but this may be because it passes his (unidentified) front door!

The parish church of Forncett St Peter

What to Expect

This route is a satisfying one to present, as despite being the longest in the book the riders' wheels never touch the tarmac of an "A" road, even to cross it. Bridges make both crossings of the busy A11 road and there is limited use of "B" roads. All roads are metalled and surfaces are better than average with less evidence of use by heavy agricultural vehicles.

Wymondham generates the traffic associated with a sleepy market town, and this is well worth enduring for the delights within the Abbey church. This ride is also the only one in the book passing the door of a convenient cycle shop if repairs or fine-tuning are pressing.

There are excellent opportunities for refreshments at the mid-point in New Buckenham, plus additional opportunities to visit pubs at several other points *en route.*

Getting Started

Starting Point: Wymondham Town Centre car park – OS Grid Ref. TM112015.

Free car parking is available in Wymondham Town Centre car park in Back Street. For train travellers Wymondham Station with its excellent connections to Norwich and London is just half a mile off the route, while Spooner Row on the same line is almost on the ride.

For those solely using pedal power the National Cycle Network runs six miles to the north-east through Norwich. The ride can easily be linked to others in the book starting with Route 1, Norwich and Tas Valley, which can be reached by cycling the three miles from Mulbarton to Stoke Holy Cross.

The Route

From the starting point in the car park in Back Lane **(1)**, Wymondham, turn left into Back Lane and follow it round until a T-junction. Turn right here in the direction signposted to Norwich A11 with Wymondham Heritage Museum directly opposite. Ride straight along Avenue Road past Avenue Garage on the right, then immediately take the right turn with The Green on your left, and ride down to the next T-junction with Myhill Garden and Pet Store straight in front of you.

Turn right here and cycle up into the centre of Wymondham past the Market Cross. This was built in 1618 after the Great Fire, which destroyed much of the town, and today contains the Tourist Information Office.

Continue riding through the shopping centre and turn left into Church Street. On the right is the chapel of St Thomas à Beckett, which was founded in 1174. The present building dates from the 15th century and after the Reformation became Wymondham Grammar School, and is today the town's library.

Church Street brings you to the Abbey church of St Mary and St Thomas of Canterbury. Wymondham Abbey was founded in 1107 and a community of Benedictine monks lived here until 1538. The dispute between the monks and the town people resulted in the unique double towers that are today such a distinctive landmark.

Leaving the Abbey turn left into the appropriately named Vicar Street and cycle away from Wymondham as the road drops down to cross the River Tilley and then over a level crossing across the disused Wymondham to East Dereham railway line.

The road then becomes Tavick Road as it climbs past the unoccupied Tavick House on the right to reach a junction at the top of the hill. Turn left at this junction **(2)** into Bradman's Lane. This brings you to another T-junction, go right and then almost immediately right again at the following T-junction which takes you out on to the main road.

There are no signposts at this junction, but turn right away from Wymondham. After a quarter of a mile, turn left off the main road **(3)** into Sawyers Lane, signposted to Suton. This lane drops down past some very pretty cottages on both sides to an unmarked T-junction. Turn left here, the road then drops down to another T-junction. Turn right here into Suton Lane.

This takes you over a level crossing and under the new A11 Wymondham Bypass towards Spooner Row. Ride past the old Chapel on the right and then straight across the crossroads in the direction signposted to Carleton Rode and New Buckenham. The Three Boars Pub on the left offers an early opportunity for a refreshment stop.

Follow this road for a mile and a half, then turn right into Upgate Street in the direction signposted to New Buckenham **(4)**. Ride along this dead straight road for three quarters of a mile to a crossroads, turn right here in the direction of Old Buckenham **(5)**.

Follow this road for two and a half miles as it skirts Old Buckenham Airfield after passing Penwood Country Chicken's Production Centre. Old Buckingham airfield is still in active use for private flying. It is hard to imagine that this quiet country area was once the base for the huge B24 bombers of the 453rd bomb group of the USAF. Among the famous Ameri-

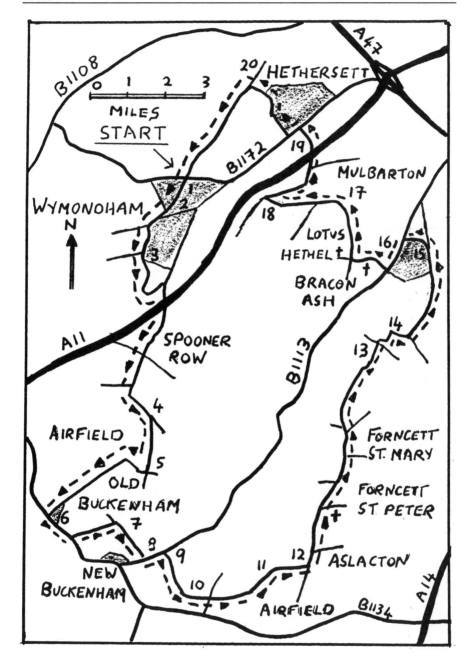

can flyers based at Old Buckenham were film star James Stewart and comedian Walter Matthau.

The road comes into Old Buckenham, passing the Secondary School on the left before reaching the famous Village Green at a T-junction. **(6)** Turn left out on to the B1077 in the direction of Diss and Winfarthing. The Ox and Plough on the left makes an excellent lunch stop with its tables out on the village green. At the time of writing, the White Horse across the road was closed for renovations.

Old Buckenham Windmill on the far side of the village green is well worth a visit. It is usually open on the second Sunday of every month between April and September, plus Bank Holiday Mondays. The mill was built in 1818 and ceased operation in 1926 and is now being restored by Norfolk Windmill Trust. Old Buckenham Windmill has the greatest outside diameter of any windmill in the UK, at 26 feet (about 8m) it is twice as wide as the average mill.

Back on to the B1077 ride in the direction of Diss and Winfarthing past Old Buckingham Stud on the left. Shortly after take a left turn off the "B" road. This is an easy turning to miss as it is not signposted. The turning has a white cottage on the right and Old Hall Farm Cottage on the left.

This well-surfaced single-track lane takes you away from the "B" road to a T-junction with Cuffer Lane. **(7)** Turn right here in the direction of New Buckenham with the church visible straight ahead.

This road passes a farm on its way into New Buckenham. After passing the parish church of St Martin's, go left at the crossroads past the village store. At the next T-junction **(8)**, go left out on to the B1113 heading out of the village in the direction signposted to Bunwell and Norwich.

Cycle straight ahead along the B1113 until the next crossroads is reached. **(9)** Turn right here into Cherry Tree Road. After half a mile turn left **(10)** off this road in the direction of Tibenham.

The road leads to a T-junction at Dove House Farm. Go left here in the direction of Carleton Rode and Norwich, and almost immediately take the unsignposted right turn off the main road into Blackbarn Road.

At the end of Blackbarn Road, go left at the T-junction on the edge of Tibenham into The Street **(11)**. This takes you past the Greyhound Pub (splendidly unsophisticated with evocative links to its wartime past) on the left, which offers an alternative venue for lunch. Shortly after this Pub turn right off this road in the direction signposted to Aslacton and Tibenham Airfield into Yule Road.

The road actually crosses the old main runway of Tibenham airfield, and to the right part of the old base is still used by an active glider club. From 1943 to 1945, the 445th bomb group of the Eight American Airforce was based here flying B-24s on bombing missions. Sadly, this base is most often remembered as being the starting point for one of the most disastrous bombing missions of the War. On the single night of 24th February 1944 122 aircrew from Tibenham were lost on a single raid over Germany.

After crossing the airfield, go left at the T-junction with Plantation Street **(12)**, in the direction of Aslacton. After half a mile, Aslacton is reached with the parish church of St Michael on the left.

Immediately after the church, take the left turn in the direction signposted to Forncett St Peter. After half a mile, the road comes to a crossroads at Pottergate Street. Go left then follow the road as it turns sharp right after crossing the River Tas in the direction signposted to Long Stratton.

Follow the road straight through as it heads in the direction of Forncett St Mary. The road heads up to a T-junction, turn right here in the direction signposted to Hapton and Long Stratton with the church of St Peter's Forncett on the right.

This particularly picturesque church has a distinctive, simple Saxon tower with portholes, while inside there is a fine 15th century archbraced roof.

Ride past the church to the end of the village and as the main road bears right, turn off left into Low Road in the direction of Hapton and Forncett St Mary village hall. The road passes Forncett Manor on the left, now a nursing home, then the Steam Museum.

Stay on this road as it bears off to the left, first becoming Spring Lane and then Bayes Lane as it heads towards Hapton. A steep downhill crosses an old railway bridge, then a stream with a farm on the left.

At the crossroads with the B1135 **(13)**, go straight across into the lane opposite signposted to Flordon. A short but sharp climb then takes you past St Martin's church Hapton on your right.

Follow the road as it bears left in the direction of Flordon and reaches a T-junction. **(14)** Go right here into The Street in the direction signposted to Flordon, then as you enter the village turn left into Long Lane opposite Black Horse Cottage with a signpost to Mulbarton.

This narrow road climbs away from the road for two miles uninterrupted riding to a crossroads on the edge of the village of Mulbarton. Go straight across this crossroads into Long Lane, which then brings you to the Village Green.

Take the left turn **(15)** which takes you down the side of the Village Green past the Primary School on the left, and then on to a T-junction with the B1113.

Go left at this T-junction in the direction signposted to Bracon Ash and New Buckenham. Ride down the B1113 for half a mile into Bracon Ash and take the right turn **(16)** by the bus shelter into School Road, signposted to Bracon Ash and Hethel churches.

Ride along School Road away from the "B" road past Bracon Hall on the right, then on the left the church of St Nicholas, which dates from the 14th century, including a font from the same period.

Beyond St Nicholas is the old primary school which, refreshingly has not become another residential conversion, but instead houses a thriving hi-fi dealership.

School Road then reaches a T-junction with Cranes Road where the ride turns right. A worthwhile detour can be taken here by continuing straight across into Church Lane, which leads to All Saints church Hethel, then returning to the School Road/Cranes Road junction. This church which dates from Norman times has a particularly peaceful setting, yet is only seven miles from the centre of Norwich. Again, it is sobering to see the memorial in the churchyard to the men of the 389th Bombardment Group of the 8th US Army Airforce who were stationed at Hethel Airfield. The memorial records how 588 aircrew were lost in action, and more pragmatically notes the total bomb tonnage dropped on enemy territory.

At the School Road/Cranes Road junction turn right out of School Road (or a left turn out of Church Lane if you made the detour to visit Hethel church). Keep straight ahead in the direction of East Carleton as Cranes Road becomes Watertower Road with the gigantic toadstool-like water tower on the left just before a T-junction. These massive water towers are a distinctive feature of the Norfolk landscape whose purpose is to provide water pressure in the flat landscape, and not as commonly thought to catch rainwater, the tops in fact being covered.

At the T-junction **(17),** turn left into Wymondham Road in the direction signposted to Hethel and Wymondham. Keep straight ahead on the Wymondham Road ignoring the left turn into Potash Lane which leads to the Lotus Car Factory (see the story of Chris Boardman's Olympic winning Lotus bike in the Cycling Agenda Section). The whole area on the left was the USAF base during the war, only part of which is occupied by the Lotus Factory and test track.

Cycle straight along Wymondham Road for two miles and then turn right into High Ash Road in the direction signposted to Ketteringham **(18)**. The road passes High Ash Farm, then after a mile bears left into the High Street, although there are no houses, let alone shops visible.

Off to the right is the church of St Peter's, Ketteringham. Beyond is Ketteringham Hall, whose chequered history included being the nerve centre for American bombing raids in the Second World War. It was also the base for Colin Chapman's victorious Team Lotus (Chapman's purpose-built East Carleton Manor is a couple of miles away and is still occupied by his family and is home to several priceless Lotus racing cars from the past).

Back on the oddly named High Street, turn off left immediately after the Ketteringham sign in the direction signposted to Hethersett into Low Street. Stay straight ahead on Low Street as it brings you to a bridge over the new busy A11 dual carriageway, then on to a T-junction with the B1172. Take care on this stretch of road as although this is a "B" road, it carries a reasonable volume of traffic.

(19) Turn out left and after a couple of hundred yards on the main road carefully take the right turn off into New Road with a signpost to Hethersett. Keep on New Road as it skirts Hethersett before coming to a T-junction with Great Melton Road.

Go left at the T-junction in the direction signposted to Great Melton, then at the T-junction at the end turn left in the direction signposted to Wymondham **(20)**.

After two and a half miles, you reach the outskirts of Wymondham at a crossroads with the B1135. Go straight across the B1135 in the direction signposted to Town Green into Melton Road. Ride straight along Melton Road until a T-junction is reached at the bottom, turn left here signposted to Little Melton (B1135).

At the next crossroads, go straight ahead here into Back Lane passing Howard Cycles on the right. A short ride up Back Lane brings you to the Car Park on the left and the starting point of the ride.

Route 3
Thetford Forest

Distance: 3+ miles

Difficulty Level: 2 to 4

Map: OS Landranger 144 – Thetford and Diss

Setting the Scene

The Brecklands are an area of East Anglia considerably less well known than the Broads or picture postcard North Norfolk.

This route comprises several rides on tracks in Thetford Forest in the heart of Breckland.

Today's Breckland landscape is very different to that of former times. Until the Middle Ages these sandy soils were productive and prized agricultural land with few trees and light vegetation. However, the rapid expansion of sheep farming caused the region to be severely overgrazed and permanent damage to the fragile ecosystem resulted.

By the end of the 19th century, the economic fortunes of the area had reached an all time low with the rearing of pheasants and other game being the sole productive activity in an area that had lost virtually all its population.

The regeneration started after the First World War with the establishment of the Forestry Commission in 1919. This new body planted Thetford Forest and other great plantations that have largely replaced the barren, overgrazed heathlands.

Thetford Forest is now a productive working forest covering 70 square miles. The bulk of the 200 000 tonnes of timber produced each year comes from Corsican pine trees, although Scots pine also play an important role as well as being the home of red squirrels.

It is ironic that in the Breckland the peace of areas such as Thetford Forest can be juxtaposed with elements of the war economy. To the north-east, lies a large Danger Area stretching as far as Watton where a preserved pre-forest landscape is scarred by ruined villages, and is still

Some quite outstanding riding . . .

violated by military training exercises. Only a short distance from the south-western boundary of the forest lies Lakenheath airfield.

As well as being a productive working forest Thetford has been sensitively developed as a recreational and educational resource and welcomes cyclists and walkers throughout the year.

Fire in this dry area is a major threat to the forest. The plantations are now defended by a criss-cross pattern of fire roads, which, in the equivalent Californian forests provided the catalyst for the development of the mountain bike. Today the fire roads of Thetford Forest are host to many descendants of those first cyclists from the slopes of Mount Tamalpais, and this area must rank along with Rutland Water as being one of the country's finest cycling resources. During the summer, cars arrive loaded with bikes ranging from children's small-wheeled models to exotic top-end mountain bikes. On one of the frequent warm sunny days, it is easy to believe you have been transported to one of the American National Parks.

What to Expect

Thetford Forest offers some quite outstanding riding, with something to suit virtually all levels of riding ability.

The riding can be divided into three main categories. First are the waymarked routes around the perimeters of the High Lodge and Brandon Park areas. These offer pleasant riding for families and cyclists of all skill levels, although the sometimes sandy track means that a mountain bike with fat tyres is preferable.

The second level of riding is represented by the fire roads that criss-cross the two forest areas. Some of these are waymarked to provide a route cutting the perimeter loops in half, but there are dozens of unmarked tracks offering riding that is more challenging. It is extremely easy to get lost on these, even when using the useful map available from the Visitors Centre. The numbered plantations can prove to be very confusing and a compass is recommended if you plan to venture off the waymarked tracks; some paths can become a maze towards the end of a ride.

The fire roads can vary from good hard packed surfaces to soft sand. There is a fair amount of loose sand and this should be treated with caution, as it is easy for the front wheel to wash out. These fire roads and tracks are suitable only for reasonable quality mountain bikes.

The third category of riding offers the most fun and challenge for the experienced mountain biker. Cutting through the forest between the fire roads in the High Lodge area are a number of well-established sections of single track, the best links four bomb holes which offer jumps and more extreme riding for the skilled mountain biker.

The Forestry Commission has accepted the use of the single track for cycling in the High Lodge area only. It is essential that just the existing well-used single tracks are followed, to keep these areas open for future cyclists, so please ride responsibly. Many of these routes derive from motor cycle endurance events and mountain bike races, giving smooth, fast, cambered tracks that follow the contours of the land; they offer some of the most exciting off-road riding in East Anglia. Some of the single tracks are technically demanding, particularly near the B1116 and are unsuitable for less experienced riders. Riding on the paths through the forest undergrowth in all areas other than High Lodge is forbidden; if you disregard this ruling you are jeopardising future access for everyone.

High Lodge Visitors Centre offers an excellent range of amenities. As well as a gift shop, cafeteria and toilets, bikes can be hired and there is a children's playground. The forest drive is open from 10.00hrs to 20.00hrs (or sunset if earlier) everyday of the year except Christmas and Boxing days. The Visitors Centre is open daily from Easter to the end of September. Check details on 01842 810271. A very useful map of the Forest cycle tracks can be bought from the Visitors Centre. The cycle-free zone immediately around High Lodge should be observed. The tracks are multi-user and cyclists should give way to walkers and horse-riders. Fire is a particular hazard in the forest; strict care must be taken to avoid any risk.

You never know what to expect!

Although some 15 miles to the east, Madgetts' Cycles in Shelfanger Road, Diss (01379 650419) is noteworthy as one of the best equipped and most helpful shops in the region. There are frequent organised cycling events in the Forest including races and reliability rides. Details are available from Cycling Club Breckland on 01603 812317.

Getting Started

Starting Point: High Lodge Visitors Centre – OS Grid Ref. TL811851.

From the A11 take the B1107 signposted to Brandon at the roundabout south of Thetford. High Lodge Visitors Centre is signposted off on the left four miles after the B1107/A11 roundabout and is approached by a Forest Drive. There is plentiful parking here but a parking fee must be paid either on entering the Forest Drive or at the Lodge.

The railway station at Brandon is only three miles from the start of the Forest Drive; take the A1065 south from the station and then left onto the B1107 towards Thetford.

The Route

The riding in Thetford Forest comprises clearly waymarked perimeter routes, interesting tracks or single track where it is clearly established.

As the perimeter cycle routes are clearly marked and the rest of the riding is largely unstructured, conventional route instructions are not given, but instead general directions are substituted.

From the car park at High Lodge the way-marked perimeter route can be picked up running parallel to the Forest Drive. If the cycle route is ridden in an easterly direction from the Lodge, you will be cycling in the same direction as cars on the parallel one way Forest Drive.

Leaving the Lodge to the east takes the rider on a six and a half mile anti-clockwise circuit of the High Lodge area, dropping downhill with a closed military area on the left, then across to run parallel to the B1116 before climbing back up to the Visitors Centre. After four and a half miles an optional left junction (opposite plantation 122) along Horse Chestnut Avenue takes you across the rather busy B1116 (Care!) and past Mayday Farm to join the six and a half mile perimeter route around the Brandon Park area.

On the High Lodge perimeter route an optional short cut, to the right, between plantations 154 and 128, just before the pond, cuts the ride in half returning the rider to the Visitors Centre.

Similarly a track at plantation 45 on the Brandon Park loop neatly halves the riding distance, but remember that riding off defined tracks is forbidden in this area.

As previously mentioned it is remarkably easy to become disoriented and lost on the unmarked tracks without a compass. It is recommended

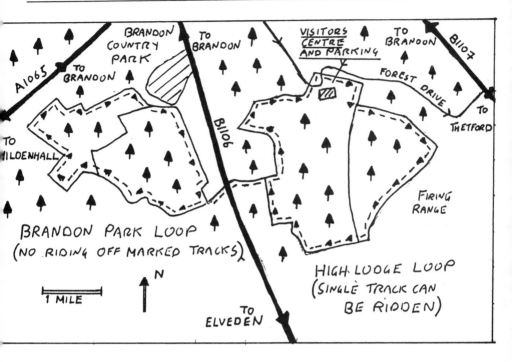

that the waymarked perimeter route is followed in either direction, away from the Visitors Centre, and that if required one of the tracks is then taken off the waymarked route. The chosen route is then followed in a straight line until it reaches the perimeter route on the far side of the area. By following a straight route, the risk of riding in disorienting circles is reduced.

The single track in the High Lodge area is more difficult to locate and it is effectively impossible to give detailed directions for this. Riding the single track between fire roads is only permitted in the High Lodge area; do not ride off the official routes in other areas as you may jeopardise access for other riders.

It is also essential to remember that tree felling may remove the single track identified in this guide. Thetford is a working forest and the topography of the area is totally changed by felling, so directions on single track may be subject to change.

The best single track starts in an easterly direction from the large bomb hole hidden in plantation 63 and swoops down to a second smaller bomb hole very close to the B1116 alongside fire route 10. The single track then heads north parallel to the B1116 in what is probably the most exciting technical riding in the whole area. The track eventually crosses fire route 11, which can be used as a route to climb back up to the starting point to repeat the whole adrenaline rush!

Another section of single track starts at the bomb hole close to the Visitors Centre in between plantation 44 and 46. This less well defined route leads to a good bomb hole complex in plantation 123 which makes a very good playground for the more acrobatic mountain biker.

These single tracks are just a small sample of many that intersect the forest. Provided that established and permitted routes are followed, there is challenging riding for keen riders. For more leisurely riding the waymarked perimeter routes and complimentary connecting rides are recommended.

Route 4
Foulsham to Reepham

Distance: 15 miles

Difficulty Level: 2

Map: OS Landranger 133 – North East Norfolk

Setting the Scene

Although only 16 miles north east of Norwich this ride offers quiet roads and timeless countryside that is ideal for leisurely and contemplative cycling.

Reepham and the surrounding area are something of a mecca for cyclists, and this ride connects with the Marriott's Way Path and the Sustrans National Cycle Network, which can be used as a backbone linking nine of the rides in this book.

In addition Route 5 in this book explores the area around Reepham off-road using the Marriott's Way for a large section of the ride and intersects twice with the current route giving the option of more extended riding in this area.

The area around Foulsham and Reepham is rich agricultural land that has been productive for many centuries. Foulsham at the starting point of the ride dates from at least the 11th century, and Guestwick church on the ride has a 12th century tower.

The de-population of Norfolk can clearly be seen from the size and number of churches in the area. Reepham had no less than three churches (one now in ruins) sharing one churchyard, while to the north of Reepham and just two miles off the ride is what has been described by an authority "as the finest church in Norfolk".

Salle church is popularly called the "Cathedral of the Fields", not just because of its unique isolated location, but also because its size would be adequate for many cities. The church is famous for many features including the nave roof and the seven-sacrament font, and is well worth visiting.

There are few conventional tourist attractions in the area. This is countryside which most tourists hurry through on their way from Norwich to the north Norfolk coast, and it is still too far from the coast to have been "gentrified" by second home owners from London. The combination of good riding, interesting landscape and unique churches make the Reepham area a secret that many cyclists hope will remain undiscovered.

What to Expect

This 15-mile ride is all on metalled, quiet, minor roads with the exception of the last mile into Reepham, which uses the busier B1145 and should be treated with care.

This is an all season ride, although there are a number of farms on the route and between Guestwick and the Themelthorpe turning in particular can be wet and mud covered in places in the winter.

There are good refreshment opportunities at the start and mid-point of the ride, but little in between. The Queens Head in Foulsham and several pubs in Reepham offer food, while the tea room at Reepham Station on the Marriott's Way Path is particularly recommended.

This route is based on a published Broadlands District Council ride, a descriptive leaflet and map is available from the Council at Thorpe Lodge, Yarmouth Road, Thorpe St Andrew, Norwich NR7 0DU.

Getting Started

Starting Point: Church of Holy Innocents – OS Grid Ref. TG032251.

The starting point for the ride is the Church of Holy Innocents in Foulsham. There is parking on the road by the church, please park with consideration for local residents.

This area is devoid of railways, the main railway through it was closed in 1984 and sections now form the Marriott's Way Path. Cyclists using the train are best served by Norwich Station, with 16 traffic-free miles along the Marriott's Way (which is also part of Sustrans National Cycle Network) leading to Reepham.

The combination of the Marriott's Way and the National Cycle Network can be used to link a number of the rides in this book, with Route 6 around Ringland a short cycle ride away down the traffic-free path.

Foulsham is used as the starting point for the ride as Reepham offers the most opportunities for a mid-ride break. However, the route can be ridden starting from Reepham (where cycle hire is available at the Old

Station, phone 01603 871187). There is a free car park in Reepham on the B1145 in Towns End, a short distance off the route.

The Route

From the starting point outside the Church of Holy Innocents in Foulsham cycle north away from the village centre with the church on your right. The parish church of Holy Innocents dates from the 14th and 15th centuries and contains some 14th century stained glass in the east chancel windows.

As you leave the village the road becomes a sunken lane and climbs to a crossroads. At this crossroads **(1)** turn right into a narrow tarmac road signposted to Guestwick and Wood Dalling. This narrow road climbs steeply uphill, and then runs across open fields to a T-junction **(2)** where you turn left again signposted to Guestwick and Wood Dalling.

From this T-junction, follow the road for a mile as it winds through undulating and very pleasant countryside to reach the Old Station House at Sheringham. This station was on the Midland and Great Northern Railway route from Norwich to Sheringham; the southern section of which now forms the Marriott's Way Path (see Route 5).

The road turns sharp left at the Old Station **(3)**, follow it round into Station Road, signposted to Guestwick and Wood Dalling. Continue along Station Road past (on your left) Guestwick Post Office located in a converted railway goods wagon — surely one of the most unusual Post Offices in the British Isles?

Beyond Guestwick Green the road turns sharp right towards Wood Dalling, do not turn right but instead continue straight ahead **(4)** signposted to Hindolveston and Melton Constable. Go

Duck if you see this sign!

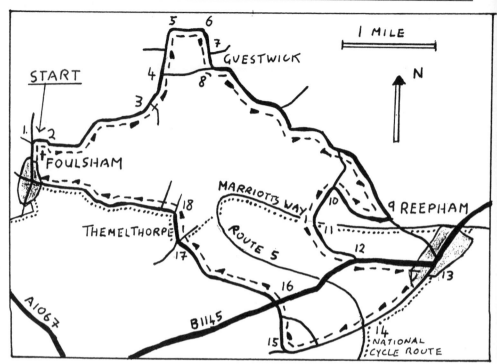

straight ahead towards Hindolveston until you reach Abbey Farm on your left, immediately after the farm buildings turn right **(5)** in to Chapel Road.

   This good single-track road goes straight ahead across open fields, follow it to the end at a T-junction **(6)** where you turn right signposted to Foulsham and Bintree.

   Shortly after the junction on the right is the parish church of St Peter's Guestwick with its distinctive square Norman tower dating from the 12th century. The rest of the church dates from the 15th century, resulting in the odd disjointed relationship between the tower and the rest of the church.

   Immediately after the church, take the left turning **(8)** into Reepham Road signposted to Salle and Reepham past the phone box. This road snakes around the field boundaries for 2½ miles of uninterrupted riding. Ahead and to the left, you will see a church and a water tower on the sky-line. This is the spire of the remarkable church of St Peter and St Paul in Salle, the 'Cathedral of the Fields', referred to in the introduction to this ride.

Closer at hand across the fields on your left is the strangely named hamlet of Odessa, perhaps a reminder of the chill easterly winds that seem to blow direct from Russia in these parts? Ignore the first right turn signposted to Themelthorpe but take the second turning **(9)** signposted to the same village. Continue along this road past Blue Tile Farm on your left and then the old workhouse cottages on your right.

Immediately after the old workhouse cottages turn left at the T-junction **(10)**, there are no signs at all at this junction. This road drops down to cross a stream, and then climb steeply through some woods to cross a disused railway on a bridge. This is part of the same Midland and Great Northern Railway seen earlier on the ride. At this point however, it has become part of both the Marriott's Way, connecting Norwich to Alysham with a 25-mile traffic-free route, and most importantly also part of Sustrans Harwich to Hull cycle route, which this ride will join for part of the return leg from Reepham to Foulsham. The path at this point is also part of Route 5 in this book; a 15-mile largely off-road ride that follows the Marriott's Way as it follows an arc around Reepham.

Almost immediately after crossing the Marriott's Way, the road ends at a T-junction **(11)**, turn left here signposted to Reepham. This road winds for a mile before reaching a T-junction with the B1145. Turn left at this T-junction **(12)** out on to the B1145 towards Reepham, and ride carefully along this relatively busy road for half a mile into Reepham.

The route turns right off the B1145 before the centre of Reepham to start the return leg towards Foulsham. However, it is worth continuing into Reepham to visit this attractive town. Continuing straight ahead takes you to the Market Place, Queens Head Pub and one of the unique features of the town, the twin churches of St Michael's and St Mary which share a common churchyard!

As well as visiting the town centre a detour following the B1145 north up Station Road to Reepham Station is also recommended. This station now stands on the Marriott's Way and has a cycle hire centre, pine workshop and excellent tea-room for a lunch break and is also the starting point for Route 5.

Back on the main route as the B1145 enters Reepham it turns sharp left up Station Road. DO NOT take the left turn but instead turn right **(13)** into School Road, signposted to Whitwell, Sparham and Great Witchingham.

This road, leading out of Reepham past the High School on the right, is part of the National Cycle Network, running steeply downhill to pass under a bridge carrying the Mariott's Way and National Cycle Network on its journey down to the centre of Norwich.

Our ride goes under the Marriott's Way, and immediately takes the right turn **(14)**, signposted to Bawdeswell. The road passes Whitwell Hall on the left and crosses open fields to a crossroads. At this crossroads **(15)**, turn right signposted to Foulsham, and continue for three-quarters of a mile past 19th-century Hackford Hall, on your left, to the crossroads. At this crossroads **(16)** go straight ahead and then bear left signposted to Themelthorpe and Foulsham.

This road continues for 1½ miles across open fields with Themelthorpe church visible ahead of you. As the road enters Themelthorpe follow it round a sharp right signposted in the direction of Foulsham **(17)**.

The ride is now again following the National Cycle Network, which has left the Old Railway track, as we now pass over on a bridge. Shortly after this bridge follow the road as it bears left signposted to Bintree and Foulsham **(18)**. Ride straight ahead on this road for 1½ miles back into Foulsham. In the village turn right in the centre into the High Street, and the church at the starting point of the ride is straight ahead.

Route 5
Reepham and The Marriott's Way

Distance: 15 miles

Difficulty Level: 1 to 2

Map: OS Landranger 133 – North East Norfolk

Setting the Scene

This is a very relaxing ride using the traffic-free Marriott's Way for two thirds of its length through the country around Reepham.

The Marriott's Way was originally a railway line linking Norwich and Aylsham, built under the supervision of chief engineer William Marriott. The line was closed in 1985 due to dwindling traffic volumes, and the route has been admirably developed by Norfolk County Council into a multi-user path linking Norwich and Aylsham.

For 15 miles from Norwich to Reepham Sustrans' National Cycle Network follows the Marriott's Way and this ride follows the National Cycle Network for the first 7 miles.

The ride follows a triangular route; two sides follow the Marriott's Way with the third linking side cutting across country on a mix of bridle ways and very quiet country lanes. Quiet cycling is the catchphrase for this road, on several sections of the railway path the absence of traffic and other noises is quite striking. This is excellent family cycling well away from the stresses and hazards of motor traffic.

There are interesting places to visit close to the route. Reepham Station at the start of the ride has an excellent tearoom, pine and gift shops, and cycle hire. 'Phone 01603 871187 for details of cycle hire.

Reepham itself has two churches plus the remains of a third all sharing the same churchyard. Cawston has a superb church with its tower faced with stone from Normandy, while two miles to the west at Salle is what is arguably Norfolk's finest church. The so-called "Cathedral of the Fields" dominates the landscape, a magnificent building and a strong reminder of the de-population of this area.

What to Expect

The Marriott's Way is a purpose-maintained path and offers excellent cycling. Use by horses however can cut it up so do not assume a continuous flat and smooth surface. Patches of loose material and some rougher riding on the bridle path section move this from an easy 1 rating to a mixed 1 to 2. A mountain bike or at least strong wheels are necessary, although road bikes are frequently seen on the railway path.

The relatively short road sections are all on quiet, minor roads. There is no continuous riding on "A" or "B" roads; however, the quiet B1145 is crossed in Cawston, and the Marriott's Way crosses the busier and faster B1145.

The first habitation reached after leaving Reepham Station is Cawston, some 12½ miles away. Although there is a pub in Cawston some self-sufficiency in food, drink and puncture outfits are recommended.

Getting Started

Starting Point: Reepham Station – OS Grid Ref. 236104.

Reepham Station is sadly now a long way from a railway. For train users Norwich Station is the best bet some 16 miles away down the traffic-free Marriott's Way and National Cycle Network.

The National Cycle Network provides an excellent route to other rides in the book. Route 4 from Foulsham to Reepham crosses sections of the Marriott's Way used on this ride twice, allowing the two routes to be combined easily.

The Route

The ride starts by joining the Marriott's Way at Reepham Station and cycling westwards away from Reepham and the gate across the path at the end **(1)**.

Ride away from the Station along the good quality track that passes over and under bridges and through cuttings. After almost 3 miles the path crosses a small lane, go straight across here continuing on the Marriott's Way on the other side. After another 2 miles the path meets the B1145 via a sharp incline. Dismount and cross with care and continue onto the path opposite.

A mile further on the path drops downhill towards a bridge under a road. Turn left **(2)** off the cycle path before the bridge, up the broadly

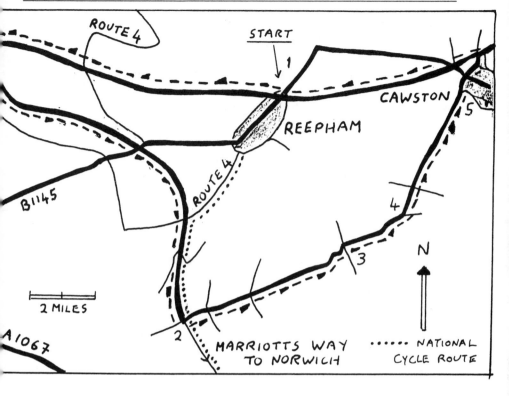

spaced steps in the direction marked with a blue Norfolk County Council bridle route sign.

At the top of the flight of steps go left onto the tarmac lane. After a couple of hundred yards on this very narrow lane go across the first junction and immediately turn left off the metalled road onto the unsurfaced track marked with the blue bridle route sign. (At the time of writing this turning was next to a particularly malodorous silage heap!)

Go straight along this unsurfaced track with cow parsley and open fields on either side. After a quarter of a mile the surface deteriorates and the track then comes to a metalled road. Go straight across and continue onto the unsurfaced track opposite.

After another half a mile this bumpy lane comes to a T-junction with another unsurfaced track, go left here. The track then reaches another metalled road, turn out left onto this road (**3**), and then after just 30 yards take the right turn, signposted to Brandiston, into The Grove.

Keep on this well surfaced lane as it winds through open fields passing a gun emplacement on the right, one wonders why this inconsequential road needed protecting? Immediately after passing Grove Farm take the left turn signposted to Cawston into Grove Lane **(4)**.

This lane then reaches a T-junction with the main road, go right here in the direction of Cawston and Marsham. Almost immediately turn off left again into Green Lane, which is signposted to Cawston.

Green Lane is now a straight ride for a mile into Cawston with the church now clearly visible ahead of you. This road brings you right into Cawston, past the church on the right to a T-junction with the High Street.

Turn right here **(5)** passing the Bell Pub (a suitable lunch stop) on the right. Immediately after the Pub turn left off the main road into Chapel Street which leads you past Broadland Winery on the right. This thriving business is a winery without any vines, unlike the vineyards passed on Route 13. Here imported grape juice is bottled mainly for the major supermarket chains. Immediately after the Winery the Marriott's Way crosses the road. Turn left off the road onto the Marriott's Way back in the direction of Reepham.

There is then an almost literally straight ride for 2 miles back along the old railway track to Reepham Station. As you ride into Reepham the path brings you to a crossing with the B1145, go straight across here onto the path on the other side. The track drops down under a bridge and through a gate to bring you back to Reepham Station and the starting point of the ride.

Route 6
Taverham and Ringland

Distance: 11 miles

Difficulty Level: 3

Map: OS Landranger 133 – North East Norfolk

Setting the Scene

This route offers some interesting riding less than six miles from the centre of Norwich. The Marriott's Way Path crosses the route and this excellent path can be used both to reach the ride from central Norwich, and to move on north east to Routes 4 and 5 in the Reepham area. The Marriott's Way at this point forms part of Sustrans' National Cycle Network, which can be used to link nine of the routes in this book into a more comprehensive tour.

The River Wensum has cut a steep valley in the Ringland area, producing some very un-Norfolk-like hills, which the route tackles as it drops to cross the Wensum. It then climbs to the higher ground to the south, before again dropping steeply to the river and finally climbing out of the valley back to the starting point.

Despite offering some appealing scenery and challenging hills this route is something of a curate's egg. The northern edges of Norwich have suffered far more from development than the southern fringes (see Route 2 starting from Wymondham as a contrast) and traffic is a persistent problem on the narrow country roads. This rural fringe is home to several golf courses and country clubs and it is not uncommon to meet Range Rovers and BMWs heading to these establishments and treating cyclists in a similar way to the pheasants which are seen (dead) at regular intervals by the roadside.

Both because of the heavy (and sometimes inconsiderate) traffic and the fairly steep hills, plus a couple of crossings of a busy "A" road, this ride is given a moderately difficult rating and is not advised for families with inexperienced or young riders. However, it is easily accessed from Norwich by bike and there is much to enjoy on the ride with the usual fine churches (particularly Ringland), some attractive scenery and several nice village pubs.

For those with catholic cycling tastes the home track of the Norwich Flyers BMX Track is just one mile off this ride in the direction of Costessey. The track is located on private ground, but the club welcomes visitors by arrangement (phone Andy Cooper on 01379 674447).

The route is based on one published by Broadland District Council, a descriptive leaflet and map is available from Broadland Council, Thorpe Lodge, Yarmouth Road, Thorpe St Andrew, Norwich NR7 0DU, telephone 01603 703266.

What to Expect

This 11-mile route is all on good tarmac roads, but it does include some of the steeper hills in Norfolk — unexceptional by the standards of other areas but a short, sharp shock treatment for those conditioned to the flatness of East Anglia.

Due to the closeness to Norwich traffic on the lanes is sometimes a problem and the two crossings of the busy A1067 need to be treated with caution.

The starting point of the ride is actually on the Marriott's Way Path and this cycle track can be used as an alternative for the first mile and last three-quarters of a mile of the ride.

There are good pubs on the ride in Weston Longville and Ringland and a general store in Taverham.

If a right is taken from the start car park in Fir Covert Road, Taverham Garden Centre will be reached with nurseries, craft workshops, a pet shop and tearoom.

Getting Started

Starting Point: Freeland Corner – OS Grid Ref. TG160166

By car: take Fir Covert Road off the A1067 — the car park is at the top of the road adjacent to the Marriott's Way.

There are no local stations; Norwich station seven miles south-east is the closest.

The route is easily accessible by bike from central Norwich: follow the National Cycle Network One signs to the start of the Marriott's Way Path, off the A1024 Norwich Inner Ring Road, alongside the Halfords store.

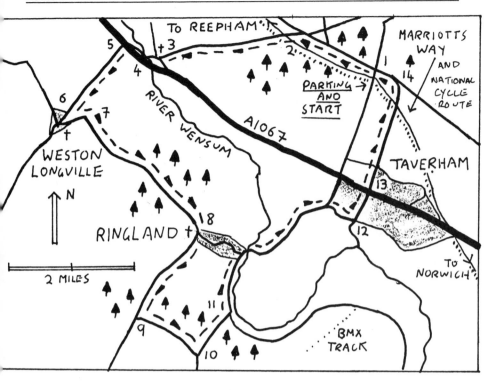

The Route

From the car park **(1)** turn out left onto Fir Covert Road, then almost immediately go left at the T-junction with the main road in the direction signposted to Attlebridge and Reepham. Ride straight ahead for a mile with the road dipping gently downhill through woods with a quarry on the left.

As the road starts to bear right, take a left turn into Felthorpe Road **(2)** signposted to Attlebridge and Lenwade. Immediately after the turn into Felthorpe Road this road crosses the Marriott's Way Path on a bridge, then drops gently downhill for three-quarters of a mile, first through woods, then open fields into the village of Attlebridge.

In Attlebridge you reach a T-junction with the 13th century church of St Andrew on your right. At this T-junction go right **(3)**, then immediately left into Old Fakenham road past the village sign.

Ahead is a bridge with a gate across it blocking the lane to cars; go through the gate and almost immediately cross a second bridge over the River Wensum, and follow the narrow path round to the right. This path reaches a side road, go straight-ahead **(4)** towards the white cottage along this side road ignoring the access to the main road on your left.

Go straight ahead into Attlebridge to the junction of the busy A1067 **(5)**. At the main road go diagonally across into Marl Hill, which is sign-posted to Weston Longville and Honingham.

The road starts to climb what is, by Norfolk standards, a reasonable hill with the church of Weston Longville coming into view straight ahead.

Go straight across the crossroads before entering Weston Longville with the Parson Woodforde pub on your right. Ahead is the 14th century church of All Saints where, in the late 18th century, Parson Woodforde was Rector and author of the widely read "A Diary of a Country Parson". Beyond the church is the perimeter of the World War II airbase used extensively by the USAAF Second Air Division for bombing raids on Germany.

After the Parson Woodforde pub and immediately before the church, take a sharp left **(6)** into Ringland Lane, signposted to Ringland. This narrow road drops down to a T-junction where you turn right **(7)**.

Go straight ahead along this rolling single-track road past Field House and Morton Hall Home Farm into the village of Ringland, arriving at a crossroads with the 14th century church of St Peter on your right. The interior of the church is well worth seeing with its fine stained glass, screen, and hammer beam roof.

At the crossroads go right and immediately left **(8)** following the sign-post to Honningham and Colton. This road goes steeply uphill past a farm, then through open fields before climbing steeply up through woods to reach a crossroads at the summit by Merryhill Leisure Pool.

Take the left **(9)** at this crossroads, signposted to Easton, the road drops downhill to a T-junction, turn left at this junction **(10)** into Ringland Road. This road drops down one of the steepest short descents in Norfolk: curb the urge to push your bike computer over 30 mph as you have to stop at a T-junction at the bottom, and turn left **(11)**, signposted to Ringland and Taverham.

This road heads back into Ringland following the River Wensum. Ride past the Swan Inn and follow the road round to the right over the River Wensum, then climb steeply with a golf course on your left between the road and the river.

At the top of the climb you pass Taverham Hall on your left (now a school) and enter Taverham, staying on the main road as it bears right then drops down through a series of bends to a crossroads.

The parish church of St Edmund's stands at this crossroads; it dates from the 14th century with a Saxon window and Norman doorway. At the crossroads turn left **(12)** into Sandy Lane, signposted to Drayton, follow this road uphill to a T-junction with the A1067.

At this junction **(13)** carefully cross the main road and go straight ahead into Breck Farm Lane opposite ignoring the cul-de-sac signs. Cycle straight up this residential lane through a short section of designated cycle path, cross the road beyond this cycle path and continue along Breck Farm Lane, which is now a road again.

Follow the lane through some farm buildings then uphill to cross the Marriott's Way Path, then ride through some smallholdings to a crossroads. Turn left at this crossroads **(14)** out on to the main road signposted to Felthorpe and Reepham. After a short distance on this road you will see on your left the car park at the starting point of the ride.

Route 7
Blofield and Strumpshaw

Distance: 7 miles

Difficulty Level: 1

Map: OS Landranger 134 – Norwich and The Broads

Setting the Scene

At only seven miles this is one of the shortest rides in the book, but it should not be ignored because of its brevity. This is classic Broadland Norfolk country dropping down the gentle slopes from Strumpshaw to the River Yare. There is lots to see and do on the ride: splendid churches, a steam museum, nature reserves and ample refreshment breaks. The riding is not challenging and is well suited to families, with the added attraction of using not one yard of "B", let alone "A" road. Access is excellent both by road and rail.

The route starts in Blofield following a ridge (all of 120 feet – 36m – above sea level) between the rivers Bure and Yare before dropping down to the Yare at Buckenham, and then following the river upstream to Brundall before climbing gently back to Blofield.

This is country that grew prosperous in the wool trade, as is evidenced by the number of churches and the size of examples such as St Andrew and St Peter in Blofield with its 110ft (33m) tower.

The area now fulfils the dual functions of commuter country for Norwich, which is only a short distance west along the A47, and holiday destination, with a large marina and several boat yards in Brundall.

What to Expect

This seven-mile ride is categorised as "easy" and can comfortably be defined as "cycling for softies". The hills are gentle but offer splendid views and some decent freewheeling on the way down. The roads are quiet and all have tarmac surfaces. The route is suitable for year round riding; the author rode it in early January after some of the most severe storms for years and all the surfaces were in fine condition.

The hazards are minor: there are three railway crossings, the un-manned one at Buckenham Station in particular should be treated with care as there are regular trains on this line. Traffic in the tourist season will be heavier; the nature reserve at Strumpshaw is a popular destination with access only from one direction along a narrow road.

There are several features on the route in addition to the attractive churches highlighted in the route description. Strumpshaw's Old Hall Steam Museum is open in the summer with its large collection of steam powered engines, fairground equipment and agricultural machinery which includes one of the country's largest working beam engines.

Strumpshaw Fen Nature Reserve is managed by the Royal Society for the Protection of Birds (RSPB) with its population including marsh har-rier, bittern and, in the winter, bean geese.

This ride follows a Broadland District Council route and a leaflet with further information is available from the Council Offices, Thorpe Lodge, Yarmouth Road, Thorpe St Andrew, Norwich NR7 0DU, telephone 01603 703266.

Getting Started

Starting Point: Blofield church – OS Grid Ref. TG 335092.

On road parking is available around Blofield church, but please show consideration for local residents.

Blofield is a short distance off the main A47 trunk road and is only seven miles from the centre of Norwich. There is excellent access by train with stations in Brundall (two!), Buckenham and Lingwood.

To make a full day's riding, this route can easily be linked to Route 8, with only four miles of quiet roads separating the two rides.

The Route

(1) From the starting point outside the church of St Andrew and St Peter in Blofield ride off to the east with the church on your right-hand side. **(2)** As you reach the outskirts of the village turn left into Shillito road just before the de-restricted signs.

(3) At the T-junction at the end of Shillito road turn right. The road heads out past Garden Farm on your left, passing some orchards and gently uphill to the crossroads **(4)**. Go straight across the crossroads in the direction signposted to Lingwood. Three-quarters of a mile after the crossroads, turn left **(5)** into Heater Lane signposted to North Burlingham and South Walsham. Cycle along this narrow single-track lane with Lingwood church visible straight ahead.

At the end of the Lane at the T-junction turn right **(6)** with the church directly opposite into Church Road signposted to Cantley and Freethorpe. The Lingwood parish church of St Peter is a fine 14th century building with interesting wall paintings and benches. Ride into Lingwood past some impressive barn conversions on the right and turn right into Vicarage Road **(7)**. Ride down Vicarage Road past the pond on your left. Further down, on your right before reaching a T-junction, there are two shops selling provisions.

Turn right at this T-junction **(8)** past the Lingwood Village sign on your right and then straight ahead with a view across the fields on the right back to Lingwood church. At the end of this road there is another T-junction **(9)**, turn left here into Chapel Road, signposted to Strumpshaw and Buckenham.

Follow this road straight ahead through some new housing, across a level crossing and then past a rare sight in rural Norfolk, a Methodist Chapel that is still in use. At the next cross roads **(10)** turn right into Norwich road, signposted to Strumpshaw and Brundall. This road takes you past the Strumpshaw village sign and into the village which has two pubs in this street. On your left is the parish church of St Peter, which dates from the 14th century.

Immediately after the church take the left turn **(11)** into Buckenham Road, signposted to Buckenham and Hassingham. After a short distance turn right into Barn Hill **(12)**. Despite being a very moderate gradient, this offers impressive views across the flood plain of the River Yare, with Blofield church at the start of the route visible to the right, and, on a clear day, Norwich visible in the distance. After the summit there is a gentle downhill to a crossroads.

At the crossroads **(13)** turn left out onto Low Road, signposted to Hassingham and Cantley. Follow this road up past the refuse disposal site (!) on your left, with a view to the right dominated by the sugar beet factory at Cantley which is almost permanently in view on Route 8.

As the road reaches a brow take a right **(14)** into Stone Road, signposted to Buckenham. This road runs agreeably downhill for half a mile with splendid views straight-ahead to the Yare. After a left bend turn right at the T-junction into Station Road **(15)**, signposted to Buckenham Railway Station, ignoring the signs which indicate this road to be a dead end. It may be for the less privileged motorist but not for the lucky cyclist.

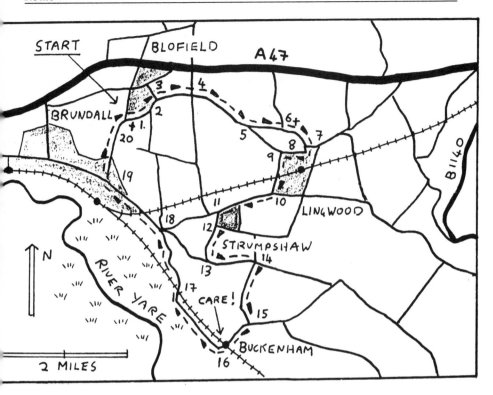

Across the field on your left can be seen the 13th century church of St Nicholas now sadly in the care of the Redundant Churches Fund – a reminder of the dramatic depopulation of these areas.

At the end of Station Road cross with extreme caution the railway line at Buckingham Station, this is an unmanned but active station with trains to Norfolk, Lowestoft and Yarmouth. Immediately after crossing the line turn right **(16)** and follow the metalled track running parallel to the railway past two cottages on the right, the first of which has a very impressive dog kennel complete with iron railings round it!

After three-quarters of a mile this track reaches another level crossing, manned this time, with the keeper's cottage on the right featuring a huge collection of garden gnomes!

Cross the railway and after 100 yards turn left **(17)** into an unmarked road immediately opposite the entrance to a farm. Follow this road as it turns right pas the entrance to Strumpshaw Nature Reserve, past some cottages to a T-junction **(18)**, turn left here and immediately left again out onto the main road, signposted to Brundall and Norwich.

This road goes straight ahead into Brundall under a railway bridge, after three-quarters of a mile reaching a mini roundabout **(19)** where you turn right into Blofield Road.

There is an optional diversion here, straight ahead at the mini roundabout and then first left to drop steeply downhill across a level crossing to a marina and some nice views of the river and water traffic.

Back on the main route on the Blofield road you ride into Blofield and the church and the starting point of the ride is visible on your right as the road starts to climb. A short distance further on, turn right **(20)** into Church Road – the starting point of the ride.

Route 8
Reedham

Distance: 10 miles

Difficulty Level: 1

Map: OS Landranger 134 – Norwich and The Broads

Setting the Scene

This easy and short 10-mile route provides pleasant riding right in the heart of the Norfolk Broads, and explores the area where the land between the rivers Yare and Bure turns into marsh. This ride is one of several in this book based on routes recommended by Broadlands District Council and is available as a leaflet from the Council, Thorpe Lodge, Yarmouth Road, Thorpe St Andrew, Norwich NR7 0DU, telephone 01603 703266.

The first part of the ride north to Wickhampton and Halvergate follows the most eastern roads in the area. To the east of these roads lie massive areas of marsh stretching as far as Great Yarmouth. The area is a very special part of Norfolk, flat, windswept, isolated and with marvellous skies. In the summer cattle graze the meadows; in the winter there is little more than wild life moving in the fields.

As with so much of Norfolk the real charm of this area is evident out of the main tourist season. Reedham is a popular boating centre for tourists, but has fortunately avoided the worst of the commercialisation seen in other Broad's centres. Reedham Ferry to the west of the village provides the only crossing of the River Yare between Norwich and Great Yarmouth for cars. The chain operated ferry links the B1140 and runs all year round, in winter a bell summons the ferry operator from his house reminding you that although you are less than 80 miles from London you have travelled a long way in time if not distance. This ride offers a great opportunity to combine cycling with a boat trip on the Broads; day boat hire is available from Sanderson Marine Craft (01493 700242) at the west-end of Reedham quay.

Rarely out of view on this ride is the huge sugar beet factory at Cantley which was built in 1912 and now processes 7000 tonnes of beet a day in the autumn harvest. Sugar beet is one of the most important crops in East Anglia and requires considerable attention before it is ready for processing in the late autumn. Large noisy lorries loaded with beet being driven with little regard for speed limits are a feature of the East Anglian country lanes in the autumn and winter, cyclists must be ready to take avoiding action as these juggernauts do not give way to mere pedal power.

This route is one of two in this area of Broadlands and as both are relatively short and easy riding a pleasant day's cycling can be had by combining this ride with Route 7 based on Blofield by cycling west from Freethorpe for five miles to Lingwood.

Apart from tourists on the Broads and lorries loaded with sugar beet this area has largely been bypassed by development, and thankfully retains much of the charm and character that has been lost to development and tourism elsewhere.

What to Expect

This is one of the easier rides in this book and it is none the worse for that. The gradients are gentle, virtually the whole route is on metalled surfaces and the busiest road used is the relatively tranquil B1140 (which can only be followed beyond Reedham if the ferry is used). Adding to the appeal are no fewer than five pubs on the 10-mile route, plus good toilets at Reedham Quay.

The good surface and gentle gradients means this "easy" rated ride is suitable for all types of bikes and can be undertaken by relatively inexperienced riders. In winter the farms can leave sections of road muddy and slippery, while conversely in summer care needs to be taken as some of the narrower roads can carry a fair amount of tourist traffic.

An optional detour can be taken from Wickhampton church out on to the marshes to Berney Arms, which boasts a railway station, windmill and a pub which is only open in the season. The route to Berney Arms is shown on the Broadlands District Council cycle map, but the last third of the metalled road is signed as private and the approach to Berney Arms follows a path marked on the ordnance survey map as bridleway. The track is poor quality and in wet weather reverts to its native marsh. Wickhampton to Berney Arms and back is 5½ miles and you can expect heavy going in wet weather. The windmill at Berney Arms is open daily from Good Friday to the end of September (01493 700605).

An "on demand" ferry link

As detailed in the "setting the scene" section, this route around Reedham can easily be combined with the nearby Blofield ride to make a pleasant day's riding.

Getting Started

Starting Point: Reedham Quay – OS Grid Ref. TG420017.

Despite its rather remote location Reedham is remarkably accessible. Many visitors arrive by boat from the river Yare, which leads to Norwich to the west, and Great Yarmouth to the east. Reedham railway station actually lies on the ride and is on the Norwich line.

For the motorist, Reedham is on the B1140, which joins the A47 to the north at Acle and the A143 to the south outside Beccles after crossing the river at Reedham ferry.

Free parking is available on Reedham Quay at the starting point of the ride. If no parking spaces are available on Reedham Quay the nearest official car park is a mile down the B1140 at Reedham Ferry. If you choose to park on the road in Reedham please show consideration to the local residents.

Refreshments and provisions are available on Reedham quay and there are excellent toilet facilities at the end of the Quay, adjacent to the pub.

The Route

The ride starts from Reedham Quay – ride east along the Quay in the direction of the railway swing bridge. At the end of the Quay follow the road to the left past the school on your right then take a right turn **(1)** into Holly Farm road. The road crosses a railway bridge, follow it as it bears left, then straight ahead for three-quarters of a mile along a narrow road with variable surface and cross the railway with care at the level crossing **(2)**.

After a short distance you will see Reedham's parish church of St John the Baptist on your right, this church dates back to the 14th century and had a thatched roof until 1981 when a major fire caused considerable damage.

Turn left **(3)** at the end of Church Dam with the entrance to Pettits Feathercraft and Animal Adventure Park on you left. Pettits is a major tourist attraction with both animals and a thriving craft centre. It is open from Easter to the end of October, but opens only on Saturdays of Bank Holiday weekends (phone 01493 700094 for full details).

This road is Halvergate Lane, follow it straight ahead as it climbs gently away from the river into open fields with Radley's sugar been factory clearly visible on your left.

Follow Halvergate Lane for almost two miles until the crossroads **(4)**. Here take a right signposted to Wickhampton into Low Road and follow this for half a mile into the village.

As you leave the village a track on the right takes you to Wickhampton, the church of St Andrew and on to the out and back route to Berney Arms described in the What to Expect section. This detour is not part of the main route and if you take it you must retrace your ride back to Wickhampton church to rejoin the main route. The church dates from the 13th century and contains some extremely good wall paintings. If the church is locked the key-holders address is displayed in the porch.

Back on the main route at the Junction **(5)** at the edge of Wickhampton take the left turn signposted to Freethorpe with the church on your right. After a short distance take the right junction **(6)**, which is un-named and un-signposted, and follow this road straight ahead for a mile into Halvergate.

As you enter Halvergate turn left **(7)** into The Street and cycle past the entrance to Halvergate Hall on your left, up to the T-junction. There is a pub a few hundred yards off the route in Halvergate if your thirst cannot wait another 1½ miles until Freethorpe. The pub can be reached by going straight past The Street and turning right at the T-junction.

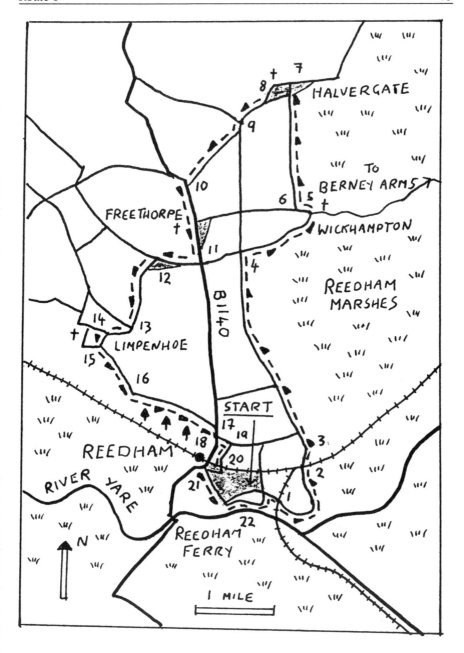

At the T-junction **(8)** turn left out on to Sandhole Road signposted to Freethorpe, Reedham & Cantley. You cycle past the 15th century church of St Peter and St Paul Halvergate partially screened by lime trees.

After the church follow the road as it bears left signposted to Freethorpe. After a short distance, with a stump of a windmill ahead of you, follow the road as it turns sharp right **(9)** signposted to Freethorpe, Cantley, the road is named Freethorpe Road.

Straight ahead for half a mile, then at the T-junction turn left **(10)** into Lower Green, signposted 'Reedham 3 miles'.

Cycle through Freethorpe with care on the B1140. At the end of the village take the right turn **(11)** signposted to Southwold and Norwich into Chapelfield leading to the Common. Immediately on your right is "The Rampant Horse" Pub which can be recommended as a refreshment break after six miles. A short distance after "The Rampant Horse" there is a general store supplying food and drink.

The route takes the left **(12)** immediately before the general stores called Old Chapel Road and signposted to Limpenhoe. This road drops down through a farm until reaching a T-junction at the bottom. At the T-junction take the right **(13)** signposted to Cantley (ignore the left to Reedham). After a short distance turn left into an unsignposted minor road called "Reedham Road".

There is a very short downhill and at the bottom take the left turn **(15)** by the White House. The road climbs uphill past an old Methodist Chapel on the right and passes through a farmyard to a T-junction **(16)** where the route turns right, signposted to Reedham.

Immediately after the T-junction follow the road round to the left. After half a mile the road reaches the B1140 at a T-junction **(17)**. At this T-junction turn out right onto the main road, signposted to Reedham. After a short distance on this road turn left into Pottles Lane, signposted to the church **(18)**.

Almost immediately, turn right **(19)** into Wotton Green. Follow this minor road across a narrow railway bridge and immediately after the bridge turn right **(20)** into a road which runs parallel to the railway to the main road with the Station on your right and the "Railway Tavern" on your left.

Turn left at the junction **(21)** into Station Road which drops towards the river and turns left. Almost immediately after this bend take the right turn **(22)** by the War Memorial, signposted "The River", this brings you back to Reedham Quay and the starting point of the route. Refreshments are available at two pubs on Reedham Quay, The Lord Nelson and The Ship.

Route 9
Litcham to Castle Acre

Distance: 21 miles

Difficulty Level: 3

Map: OS Landranger 132 – North West Norfolk

Setting the Scene

This route offers some fine riding, good meaty stretches of uninterrupted cycling connecting charming villages with good pubs, and excellent churches and antiquities. The linking thread of the National Cycle Network lies to the north, but there are connections to other rides in this book.

Castle Acre probably has more history to offer than any other single site in East Anglia, with a Norman Castle, medieval priory and 15th century church all within a square mile. Contrasting with the popularity of Castle Acre are some of the less-known and quieter villages such as Great Massingham and Little Dunham, backwaters of rural Norfolk and retaining much of their charm with far fewer visitors than the sometimes extremely popular Castle Acre.

This is the highest area of Norfolk; Little Dunham Lodge

Castle Acre

is supposedly the highest Great House in Norfolk, while the route passes the highest spot heights in the county. This high ground is the chalk backbone of East Anglia topped by clay, and this is a countryside of big farms and wide-open fields. The high ground covered in the first part of the ride around Little Dunham is the watershed between three of Norfolk's rivers, the Wensum to the east, the Nar to the south, and the Wissey in the west.

What to Expect

This route gives the author considerable satisfaction as in the entire 21 miles not a single "A" or "B" road is followed (except at inevitable crossings). The rating of difficulty (3) is based on the length, and the fact that Castle Acre can be thronged with tourist traffic in the summer. Other than this the route is simple cycling pleasure. The whole route is on tarmac roads and there are only a couple of very short sections where local farmers try to spoil the cyclists' day by covering the surface with mud and dirt.

In simple terms the ride consists of four very attractive villages linked by excellent cycling. Each of the villages offers at least a pub; others such as Castle Acre and Linham offer several shops and tearooms.

Getting Started

Starting Point: Letcham Common Nature Reserve car park – OS Grid Ref. TF888173.

This car park is just out of Litcham on the Little Dunham road. King's Lynn offers the nearest railhead, 16 miles bike ride to the west.

Route 10 (Little Walsingham to Burnham Market) can be reached by riding to North Creake, some 13 miles north, and then linking with the National Cycle Network, while Routes 4 and 5 around Reepham lie some 10 miles to the east.

The Route

The ride starts from the car park at Letcham Common Nature Reserve (1). Leave the car park and turn right heading towards Great and Little Dunham. The route gently weaves through the countryside with woods on the right, then through open countryside for two miles to reach the church of St Andrew's on your left.

St Andrew's church, Great Dunham, is one of the most complete Saxon churches in Norfolk. It has been used continuously for worship for more than a thousand years, while on the south side below the 19th cen-

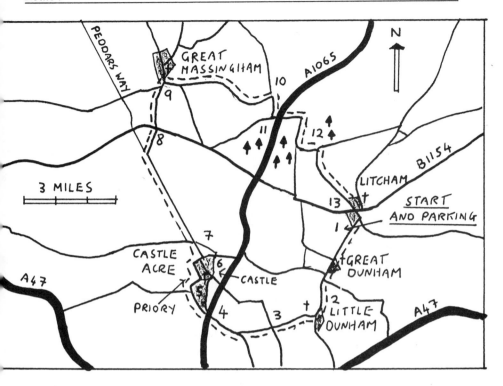

tury window is part of an arch formed of Roman tiles. The heritage of this region is underlined by the fact that sermons have been delivered from the pulpit here for more than 300 years, baptisms have used the font for 600 years and worship dates back more than a millenium.

From the church continue on the main road and leave the village in the direction signposted to Little Dunham and Swaffham. After a mile of cycling through open countryside Little Dunham is approached over a bridge crossing a disused railway line.

After passing the sign for Dunham Museum on your right turn right **(2)** into The Street signposted to Sporle and Swaffham. Over on the left of the main road is Little Dunham Lodge, supposedly the highest located (345ft, 105m) Great House in Norfolk. So gentle is the terrain in this county that it is claimed that the spires of Norwich and Ely Cathedrals, and shipping at King's Lynn have been seen from the roof. The Lodge is a splendid Georgian house, and one of several famous occupants was the poet William Cowper who provided the words for the hymn "God moves in a mysterious way".

One hundred yards down the street on the left is the Black Swan, which offers an early refreshment stop. Keep on The Street as it bears right immediately after the Black Swan and leaves the village past the Old Schoolhouse on the right, followed by St Margaret's church, a relatively newcomer from the 13th century compared with its neighbour in Great Dunham.

Visitors to East Anglia wonder at the number of churches, and are told that in medieval times this was a densely populated county. Here in Little Dunham there is visible evidence. On the far side of the church drive, in the meadow to the west, can be seen the humps and bumps which are the earthwork remains of the medieval village which once surrounded the church.

Leaving behind St Margaret's ride away from Little Dunham on the road east towards Castle Acre. Again the route crosses upland agricultural country bridging the disused railway line again before coming into the hamlet of Sporle. Go straight ahead at the crossroads here **(3)** in he direction signposted to South Acre. The route now follows the appropriately named (but misspelt) Peddars Way all the way through to Great Massingham.

The road drops in a lovely downhill towards the A1046, with Castle Acre and the ruined Priory visible ahead. The road reaches the A1046 **(4)**, cross it diagonally to the right in the direction signposted to South Acre. The Peddars Way climbs away from the "A" road, and as you reach the top of the climb you can see Castle Acre spread out across the fields to your right with the church and ruined castle clearly visible ahead.

The road drops downhill, and at the bottom of the hill as the road bears left take the right fork **(5)**, which is signed "Ford" and 'unsuitable for motors'. After a short distance down this narrow lane the road turns right around a farm, and there is a short distance of poor road surface. Across the river on the left the ruins of the Priory can now be seen clearly.

The track reaches the River Nar at a broad ford crossed by the pedestrian bridge on the left-hand side. Stop half way across the bridge to enjoy the panorama of water and medieval ruin, probably the most striking view you will see on any ride in this book.

The ruins of Castle Acre Prior are probably the finest in East Anglia. The well preserved west front of this medieval monastery is the outstand-

ing feature, still making a bold statement with its original Norman structure embellished with later additions.

From the ford climb on the well-surfaced lane towards the church
reaching a T-junction **(6)** at the top. The route turns right at this junction,
but a diversion to visit the Priory can be made by turning left. The ruins are
now under the management of English Heritage and there is an entrance
fee. There are refreshments, a gift and bookshop. At the top of the car
park there are free toilets and a water tap.

From the T-junction take a right **(6)** to follow the main route into the
centre of Castle Acre. On the right is the largely 15th century church of St
James The Great. There are many interesting features in the church, but
the most memorable is perhaps the 15th century hexagonal font with its
towering cable operated cover.

Past the church is the village centre with two pubs, tearooms and several shops. Ride through the village centre to the junction at the end **(7)**
where you go straight ahead in the direction signposted to Massingham
and Rougham.

As the road leaves the village it passes the entrance to the castle on
the right. The castle is of Norman origin, but other parts of the site date
back as far as the Iron Age.

Keep straight ahead on the road out of the village passing the recre-
ation ground on the right and then out into open fields ignoring the various
turnings off the road to Massingham. This is The Peddars Way which follows a Roman Road in a dead straight line for three and a half miles before going on to Great Massingham for another one and a half miles. Over
on the left at the end of the straight section is some of the highest ground
in Norfolk with a 95 metre spot height being shown on the Ordnance Survey Map.

After bearing right the road drops and then climbs to a crossroads with
the B1145, go straight across **(8)** here in the direction of Great
Massingham, which is reached a mile further on. Ride into the village until
you reach the junction before the very pretty village pond.

The route turns right at this junction, but carrying straight on makes a
worthwhile diversion to the Rose and Crown pub and restaurant. The Village Green, which is one of the largest in Norfolk, has two duck ponds
and a parish church. The outstanding feature of St Mary's church is the
13th century early English porch, while the finely proportioned tower is 15th
century perpendicular period.

The main route turns right **(9)** before the pond signposted in the direction of Weasenham. Follow the Weasenham road out of the village past the Old Wesleyan Chapel on the left, which is now being converted into a house and pass a third duck pond – is this a record?

This is a straight ride for three and a half miles following the signposts in the direction of Weasenham St Peter. On the skyline to the left are the hangars of the now-disused West Raynham airfield. This base was unusual in this area as it did not host a USAF squadron in the war, but was the home to RAF Blenheim squadrons.

As the road enters the village of Weasenhall take the first right **(10)** into Dodma Road, go straight ahead along this road, ignoring Church Lane on the left, which leads to the church of All Saints Weasenham.

At the end of Dodma Road take a left at the T-junction, this brings you immediately to the A1065. On the right is the Ostrich Inn, with the chimneys of Weasenham Hall visible through the trees on the right.

Go diagonally across the A1065 **(11)** into the road opposite and then after a few hundred yards take the right turn signposted to Lexham. This road takes a sharp right out past High House Farm where the surface can be treacherous, courtesy of the resident farmer.

The road then goes straight ahead, and after passing through a wood reaches a crossroads **(12)**. Go left at this crossroads in the direction signposted to Litcham and Tittleshall. Stay on this road as it bears round to the right signposted in the direction of Litcham, passing the entrance to High House Farm on your left, and then after one and a half miles the outskirts of Litcham are reached and you come to a T-junction.

At this junction go right **(13)** into Pound Lane which is signposted to Litcham and Swaffham. Ride into Litcham and at the next T-junction turn right **(14),** signposted to Beeston and Dunhams.

Keep going down through the village centre with the Ball Public House on the left, heading in the direction signposted to Dereham and Swaffham. Immediately after Old Litcham School on the left is All Saints church. The chancel rood screen dating from 1436 is undoubtedly the highlight of the church. The screen is well restored and complete. The church largely dates from the 15th century, but the tower was added as a present from a wealthy local tanner in 1669.

Beyond the church are a Post Office, village store and high school which caters for a large catchment area in the surrounding countryside.

Ride out of the village and take the right turn signposted to Great Durham. 100 yards beyond this turning on the right is the entrance to the car park from where the ride started.

Route 10
Walsingham to Burnham Thorpe

Distance: 21 miles

Difficulty Level: 3

Map: OS Landranger 132 – North West Norfolk

Setting the Scene

This glorious 21-miler follows the National Cycle Network from Little Walsingham to Burnham Thorpe for 12 miles before returning via North Creake Abbey.

History and religion feature strongly in this ride. It starts from Little Walsingham with its famous shrine which in medieval times was known as the Nazareth of England, while half way round the ruins of the 13th century North Creake Abbey are well worth visiting.

Mid-way on the ride is Burnham Thorpe, the birthplace of East Anglia's most famous son, Lord Nelson. The site of his birthplace is marked, and an Inn with strong connections to him offers one of the best lunch stops of any of the rides in this book.

The landscape of this ride is formed from boulder clay and chalk, which makes the rolling backbone of East Anglia, and contrasts with the low-lying Fen and Broadland areas. The ride back from North Creake to Little Walsingham crosses a peaceful upland (by Norfolk standards!) area, which is very different from the often busy nearby north Norfolk coast.

One of the many attractions of this ride is that it offers a traffic-free detour into Wells next the Sea. This is part of the National Cycle Network, and is one of the few opportunities that cyclists have to reach the north Norfolk coast without having to venture onto the busy and crowded coastal roads.

The ride also gives easy access to Holkam Park and Hall. This great Palladian-style house has remained virtually unmodified since completion in 1762, and the attractions include free car parking, a garden centre and pottery.

Little Walsingham is now the only shrine in England, and this means that in the Pilgrimage season from May to October the village and surrounding area can become very busy, while the Burnhams become home to weekend residents from Hampstead and Islington. At any time of year, however, this ride will reward, and a bonus is a section of traffic-free riding, courtesy of Sustrans and the National Cycle Network.

What to Expect

This ride is rated 3 for difficulty; not because of any major difficulties, but rather due to its 21-mile length and its use of a mile of the B1355. In summer, this suffers from the likes of Range Rovers being driven quickly by media types commuting between their weekend cottages on the fashionable North Norfolk Coast and Hampstead.

More than half of the ride is on the bike-friendly National Cycle Network, which has the additional bonus of excellent signposting. The Sustrans route also delivers two continuous miles of traffic-free off-road riding. This section is rideable by a mountain bike all year round; however, a tarmac alternative is also available. A short section of the off-road track can be muddy in winter but remains rideable.

The ruins of 13th century Creake Abbey

The ride also offers more earthly alternatives to religion and history. Pubs are located in Little Walsingham, Wighton and North Creake, but the gem is the Lord Nelson in Burnham Thorpe. This Inn dates back to the 1650s and was the scene in 1793 of his leaving party before taking command of his new ship. As well as connections with Lord Nelson the pub is also notable for the absence of a bar, this does not however prevent the serving of excellent food and drink.

Getting Started

Starting Point: Little Walsingham car park – OS Grid Ref. TF933369.

The most attractive access is to use the National Cycle Network, which passes through Little Walsingham and connects with other rides in the book. Car users should park in the car park in Little Walsingham. Beware, however, that the throng of visitors to the Shrines means this is not a free car park (pray and display?). Allow adequate time for the ride and lunch at the Lord Nelson.

Sadly, north Norfolk is the region that the railway forgot – the nearest railheads are some distance off in King's Lynn, Cromer and Norwich.

The Route

The starting point of the ride is the main car park in the centre of Little Walsingham (pay and display – see getting started).

Proceed down towards the village centre by **walking** down the "**No Entry**" road out of the car park. At the bottom of this one way road **(1)** at the T-junction turn left into the one way signposted to Wells and Walsingham Light Railway and ride up this street away from the village centre.

At the top of this street **(2)** turn right at the T-junction opposite the Robin Hood Inn in the direction signposted to Wighton and Wells into Guild Street, following the National Cycle Network marker. After 100 yards, turn left at another T-junction out on to the main road called Wells Road and again signposted to Wighton and Wells.

After a short distance turn right **(3)** off the main road into St Peter's Road, following the National Cycle Network marker. This road leads, past bungalows on your left and a playing field on your right, out of the village on a well-surfaced single-track road. This road passes the church of St Peter's on the left and drops down to a T-junction. At this junction **(4)** turn right, there is no signpost or road name. Shortly after this junction, there is a ford with a pedestrian bridge for the less adventurous. Follow the road gently uphill to the T-junction in the pretty village of Great Walsingham.

Turn left here **(5)** into Scarborough Road signposted in the direction of Bingham, then it is slightly uphill for a very short distance before turning left again in the centre of the village. This left turn is not signposted or named, but has a clear National Cycle Network marker and takes you past Shepherds Cottage on the left. This road climbs away gently uphill with rolling fields on either side, then through tall hedgerows and after a mile enters the village of Wighton.

At the T-junction **(6),** turn left following the National Cycle route in the direction of Wells. The road drops down to enter the second part of the village following the High Street pas the Carpenters Arms Pub then uphill past All Saints church on your right and the Old School House on the left, now an Art Gallery.

At the top of the High Street **(7),** turn right at the T-junction in the direction signposted to Wells. (If you want to stay on tarmac take the left turn here and ride for three miles to rejoin the route at New Holkham.) After the right at the T-junction, ride straight ahead ignoring the left turn mentioned above, and pass the pond where the road bears right. At this point, take left into the unmetalled track signed "unsuitable for motor vehicles" and marked with By-Road and National Cycle Network signs. This rough track climbs past a solitary graveyard on the right and continues uphill for 1½ glorious traffic-free miles to reach a junction at a solitary cottage creepily named Gallow Hill.

The right fork here is a convenient extension of the National Cycle Network that reaches the centre of Wells next to the Sea along one mile of off-road riding. The main National Cycle Network takes the left fork here **(8),** and immediately follows what in winter can be a short wet and muddy section. This is still rideable, as fortunately there is a firm surface under the mud. The wet conditions only last for 100 yards and is then replaced by a good, firm hard-core track which leads downhill to meet a tarmac main road, the B1105.

Go straight across the B1105 **(9)** into the road opposite, which is signposted to New Holkham and bears away to the left and the National Cycle Network. Continue straight ahead on this road with the flint wall of Holkham Hall estate on your left. After 1½ miles take the right turn **(10)** by the red phone box, following the signposts for Burnham Thorpe and the National Cycle Network, with the flint wall on the right.

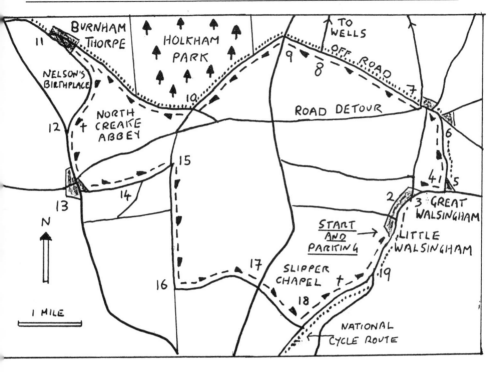

This road is a straight 2½ miles into Burnham Thorpe, and if you have got your timing right a good lunch. After a quarter of a mile you pass the entrance of Holkham Park on your right with a view to the Obelisk, while on the left is the Triumphal Arch.

The road then starts to drop downhill with superb views across to the coast with churches and windmills forming high spots in the panorama. There then follows what, by Norfolk standards, is a good fast downhill which rapidly brings you into Burnham Thorpe. Cycle through the village, ignoring the first signpost to North Creake, until you reach the Lord Nelson Pub on the left. The Lord Nelson is highly recommended as a lunch stop (see What to Expect).

Back on the ride, continue away from the Lord Nelson and out of the village into open country before reaching a T-junction **(11)**. Go left signposted to North Creake (the National Cycle Network goes right towards Burnham Market). After a mile, you pass the site of Nelson's birthplace on the right. The house where Nelson was born no longer stands, instead a more recent Rectory is in its place. The road climbs straight ahead to a

Replica of the Virgin of Walsingham in the Holy House at Little Walsingham

T-junction **(12)** with the B1355, where a left is taken onto the main road in the direction signposted to Fakenham.

A lane off on the left at this junction leads down to North Creake Abbey, which should not be missed. North Creake Abbey was founded as a hospital towards the end of the 12th century and was converted to an Augustian Priory in 1206 and an Abbey in 1231. It was dissolved in 1506 after the Abbot and Cannon had died, probably of the plague. The remains of the Abbey include the 13th century presbytery and transept, and a large chapel added east of the north transept in the 14th century. The remains of the Abbey are marvellously evocative, particularly out of season when their serenity and peacefulness can be fully appreciated.

From the junction ride along the B1355 into the village of North Creake with the Jolly Farmer Pub on the right in the village centre. As you reach the end of the village take the un-signposted left turn called Roadhill opposite the Old Post Office, which has a GR post box on the front wall **(13)**.

This road climbs sharply uphill away from the "B" road before levelling off and crossing rolling open countryside which is very different from the conventional image of Norfolk as a county of water and windmills. Ride past ruined farm buildings on your left and after a mile turn left at the T-junction **(14)** with the old quarry workings on your left.

Continue until reaching the turning on your right; take this turn signposted to Fakenham **(15)**. Follow this road as it goes straight ahead for 1 ¼ miles, you are now following the Old Roman Road, which is dead straight. The road climbs gently uphill to a crossroads go straight-ahead signposted to Waterden.

The Old Roman Road has a smooth tarmac surface and drops down a good downhill, which ends at a T-junction. **(16)** Go left here signposted to Barsham and Walisingham. Climbing uphill, pass the exquisite Old Rectory and church on the left.

After the Old Rectory the road climbs quite steeply past Waterden Farm on your left, and then flattens out to cross open fields to the crossroads with B1105. At these crossroads **(17)** go straight ahead into the lane marked "By Road", which drops downhill to the right to North Barsham. Take the left turn **(18)** signposted to Walsingham Slipper Chapel and RC Shrine, and ride out of the village past another exquisite church on the left. After passing through a redundant railway bridge the road reaches the Roman Catholic Shrine of Our Lady of Walsingham.

Since 1061, this shrine has been a constant reminder to pilgrims and travellers of the peace and joy of the Christian Gospel. The medieval shrine was destroyed in the religious conflicts in the 16th century, but Catholics and Anglicans together have restored the shrine and its pilgrimage. The ancient Slipper Chapel is the Catholic Shrine, and there is an Anglican Shrine in the village of Little Walsingham.

Ride past the Shrine and follow the road as it winds along with a stream on your right, reaching a T-junction with the main road. Go left at the T-junction **(19)** in the direction signposted to Walsingham, and almost immediately you are back in Little Walsingham at the start of the ride. Ride straight ahead into the village and follow the signs to the car park.

Route 11
Bungay and The Godric Way

Distance: 24 miles

Difficulty Level: 3

Maps: OS Landranger 134 – Norwich and The Broads;
OS Landranger 156 – Saxmundham

Setting the Scene

Much of the attraction of Bungay today is because the town and its imme-diate surroundings are not part of the Broads waterway network, thereby saving the town from the worst of the excesses that define Wroxham and other Broads towns.

Although Geldeston Lock some 8 miles downstream is now the limit of navigation, in earlier times trading wherries carried wool and other car-goes from Bungay to the sea at Lowestoft, then on to the far reaches of the British Isles and across the North Sea to the low countries.

It is the River Waveney that gave the town both its name and historic importance. "Bongue" means good ford and Bungay was an important crossing point for the Romans with one of their major routes, Stane Street, running through the town.

Today Bungay's economy is based on tourism, agriculture and light industry. There is a long tradition of printing in the area and the first edi-tion of Alice in Wonderland was printed here. The printing tradition is car-ried on today by several presses, notably Clays on the edge of the town.

The River Waveney also defines the geography of the area with the predominate flatness of South Norfolk changing to the gentle gradients of North Suffolk. To the South of the town is the bleak and beautiful upland plateau known as the Saints and crossed by this route.

The Saints is so-called because virtually every village in the area is named after a Saint, including St Peter South Elmham the site of St Pe-ter's Brewery which is passed by the Godric Way Cycle Route.

St Peter's Hall dates from around the 11th century and includes a moat built as a defence against raiding Vikings. The Hall was rebuilt in the 16th century using monastic salvage, but in the 20th century its fortunes waned as the wool based local economy declined. In 1996, the Hall re-opened as a brewery using the excellent water from its own borehole and with state of the art brewing equipment in the outhouses. Today, St Peter's is a thriving brewery, an excellent restaurant and a visitors centre. The beers are all "real ales" including "traditional" beers – bitters, milds etc – as well as some more unusual beers such as honey porter and fruit beer. The brewery makes an excellent break on the Godric Way, phone 01986 782322 to confirm opening times.

The once-bustling River Waveney can now be peacefully explored by rowing boat or kayak, hired from Outney Meadow Caravan which is situated a short distance off the cycle route near the A143 and B1332 junction. Phone 01986 892338 for details.

On the southern edge of the town on the A144 is the excellent Waveney Valley swimming pool with a water chute and learners' pool. This bright, airy and rarely crowded pool offers a refreshing end to a circuit of the Godric Way, phone 01502 523452 for more information.

In many ways, this route epitomises the real spirit of East Anglia away from the main tourist centres. It passes through productive farming country, past grand halls, houses and churches that have been left peacefully stranded by an economy that has shifted its power base well away from this once prosperous area.

What to Expect

The Godric Way is a 24-mile waymarked route looping around Bungay. The route is a joint project between Bungay Town Council and the Godric Cycling Club and a route leaflet is available from the Town Tourist Office. Waymarking is helpful but at times sporadic.

Although the route is mostly on tarmac, some of the roads are narrow, poorly surfaced and there are (by East Anglian standards) some moderate hills. Although eminently rideable by a moderately accomplished cyclist, it is not recommended for beginners or families with younger riders. In particular the four crossings and short sections on the busy and fast A143 and A144 should be treated with extreme care.

This route is one of the few in the book that uses an "A" road. It is not possible to avoid using the A144 for a short distance unless a major detour is made to the south. The A144 is relatively quiet, and is followed for half a mile before the route leaves it for quieter by-roads.

The excellent Madgetts' Cycles in Diss (see Route 3 for details) is 15 miles to the west. The route has few refreshment breaks, but what it loses in quantity it more than makes up for in quality. St Peter's brewery has already been mentioned and the Black Swan in Homersfield offers an excellent selection of food and drink at the mid-point of the route.

Because of its length, hills, variable surfaces, but primarily because of its use of short stretches of busy "A" road, the Godric Way is rated Level 3 (out of a maximum of 4) in difficulty. However, as the route follows an anti-clockwise circuit of Bungay numerous "short circuit" options are available back to Bungay. In fact, the route never wanders more than 5 miles from the town centre.

Getting Started

Starting Point: Bungay Town Centre – OS Grid Ref. TM337898.

Bungay is 12 miles south east of Norwich at the intersection of the A143 and A144. The nearest railway station is Beccles. However, Diss, 16 miles to the west along the not recommended for cycling A143 is on the main London line.

The route directions start from the town centre and follow an anti-clockwise circuit in the same direction as the way-markers, but note there are two variations from the marked route.

There are several pay and display car parks in the town centre. Free on-road parking is available on the town's outskirts. Please show consideration for local residents.

The route follows the National Cycle Network for a short distance, and this offers an excellent connection to a number of other routes in this book, including Route 1 (Norwich and Tas Valley) to the north and Route 12 (Peasenhall to Wissett) to the south.

The Route

From the starting point in Bungay Town Centre (1) follow Prior Street, signposted to B1062 Beccles, with the circular Saxon tower of Holy Trinity church on your left. At the T-junction, turn left into Staith Road, which leads into Beccles Road.

After a quarter of a mile, take the left (2) after the Watch House Pub. The left turn has two forks, take the right road "Low Road" not Wainford Road. Follow Low Road (3) for one mile before turning left at the signpost to Ellingham; the road crosses Benstead Marshes for a quarter of a mile

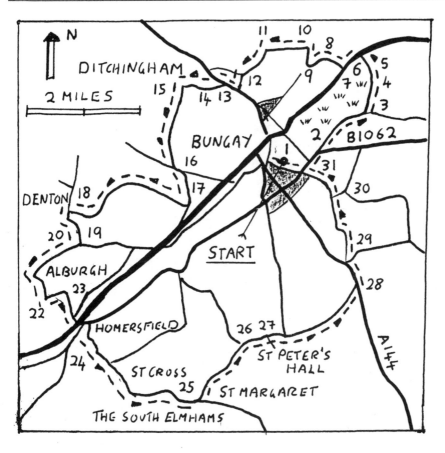

before crossing the River Waveney at the very picturesque Water Mill. Immediately after the Mill **(4)** take the unsignposted left turn into Old Station Lane. The road starts to climb away from the River. At the T-junction **(5)** turn left and follow the road as it bears left until it joins the busy A143, signposted to Broome and Bungay. Turn left **(6)** onto the A143 and ride through Ellingham for a short distance. Carefully turn right **(7)** across the oncoming traffic into Home Farm Road. This road climbs away from the River. Turn left at the T-junction **(8)** and cycle past Ivy House Farm. Before the road crosses Broome Beck **(9),** take the right turn into Church Lane, signposted to Thwait.

The last feeling of being on the edge of a town is lost as this narrow road climbs gently past Broome Place. On your right is an imposing house that reminds us of the former prosperity of this area. The road now comes to a T-junction **(10)** with Broome church opposite you across the fields. This view is quintessential East Anglia, a splendid church outlined against the sky with not a house in sight; Broome church is in fact almost a mile from the eponymous village! At the T-junction turn left, signposted to Thwait and Hedenham. Follow this single-track road for three-quarters of a mile, there is a comparatively rare Norfolk downhill – short, sharp and winding with some loose surface – so treat with caution.

At the end of the road **(11)** turn left and then almost immediately right out onto Belsey Bridge Road. Ride past All Hallows convent in its peaceful setting above Ditchingham. Pass the Convent **(12)** and turn left after St Mary's church, Ditchingham, and drop down to a T-junction on the B1332. Turn right **(13)** out onto the B1332, signposted to Hedenham, and then left into Pound Lane, signposted to Earsham. Follow the signposts to Earsham **(14)** as the road drops down to a T-junction where your turn left out onto a wider road, again signposted to Earsham. Cycle straight-ahead **(15)** along this road for one mile passing through Great Wood halfway along.

Immediately after leaving the wood, you will see the magnificent Georgian wing of Earsham Hall on your right. This imposing house is now used in part for a thriving pine workshop and showroom and is well worth a visit. (Phone 01986 893423 for opening hours.)

After Earsham Hall **(16)** take the second left into Pheasants Walk and after half a mile take the first right. At this point **(17)**, the route leaves the Godric Way for three miles. The Waymarked route inexplicably includes two avoidable and dangerous crossings of the A143, which are avoided by turning right off Pheasants Way and heading up towards Denton. The only advantage of the waymarked route is that if Pheasants Way is followed down to the A143, the Otter Trust is reached by crossing the fast and busy main road and cycling back half a mile along the old parallel road towards Bungay.

The Otter Trust, with its almost natural habitats for otters and other wildlife is well worth a visit (phone 01986 893470 for further information), but beware of crossing the road.

The detour off the Godric Way take a right from Pheasants Walk and follows the road past three farms for two miles before reaching a crossroads on the outskirts of Denton. Take a left at this T-junction **(18)** and a right at the next T-junction **(19)** after half a mile into Alburch Road you get back on the waymarked route.

The road continues climbing until you reach a left fork **(20)** into School Road, signposted to Redenhall and Harleston. At the next crossroads **(21)** turn left into Low Road, signposted to Wotwell. After a quarter of a mile **(22)**, turn left into Station Road, signposted to Homersfield and Bungay. The road drops downhill to the A143, approach this junction with caution. Proceed with care **(23)**; turn right onto the main road, signposted to Harleston, almost immediately take the left turn signposted 'B1062 Homersfield'. Ignore the next right turn and look for a track on the right **(24)**, which takes you across the old bridge (now closed to traffic) into Homersfield. The Black Swan on your left is an ideal venue for lunch, or alternatively, the banks of the Waveney are excellent for picnicking.

Leave the Pub cycling away from the River and take the right turn, signposted to Bungay/Harleston. Follow the road straight ahead, signposted to Halesworth, as it climbs steeply away from the river, again disproving the myth that East Anglia is all flat! Ignore the various side turnings on this straight road and keep climbing into the village of St Cross South Elmham on to St Margaret South Elmham. At the far end of the village **(25)** turn left, signposted to St Peter's, and follow this narrow, winding road as it climbs to a T-junction. At this T-junction **(26)**, turn right, signposted to St Margaret's Ilketshall. Turn left at the next T-junction **(27)**, signposted to St Margaret's Ilketshall and St Lawrence. After half a mile you will see St Peter's Brewery on your left – an excellent diversion for lunch or a tour of the brewery (bookings advisable on 01986 782322).

Follow the road straight ahead through Ilketshall St Margaret and then on for another half a mile until you reach the A144 junction. Turn left onto the main road **(28)**, signposted to Bungay, and cycle carefully along the A144 for about half a mile before turning off to the right. At this right turn, take the immediate left fork **(29)**, signposted to Mettingham Castle. This winding road drops downhill for $1\frac{1}{2}$ miles to bring you back to the outskirts of Bungay.

Half way along a detour to the right **(30)** and right again takes you to Mettingham Castle. Only the gatehouse, towers and remnants of a Barbican remain of this 14th century castle.

Back on the main route **(31)**, at the bottom of the hill, turn right at the T-junction and then almost immediately left out onto Beccles Road which leads you back into Bungay Town Centre and the completion of the route.

Route 12
Peasenhall to Wissett

Distance: 19 miles

Difficulty Level: 3

Map: OS Landranger 156 – Saxmundham

Setting the Scene

This route explores the heart of north-east Suffolk and is well distanced both from the popular coastal area and the busy A140 road. The relative quietness and solitude of this ride are one of its main appeals. In 19 miles after leaving Peasenhall there are just two pubs, both mean making detours from the main route, and no shops or tea rooms, so self-sufficiency is the order of the day.

This is still a productive agricultural area and pig farms, orchards and arable land all feature on the ride. This used to be rich wool producing country; the churches and houses such as Heveningham Hall indicate the region's affluent past.

The ride shares the common link of the National Cycle Network with many of the other routes in the book with the last seven miles back to Peasenhall following Sustrans' Hull to Harwich route. At the time of researching the National Cycle Network was not signed at all in this area. However, subsequently Suffolk County Council has allocated money to marking the route, so hopefully the reader will find adequate marking.

The terrain here is an upland (by Suffolk standards) plateau 150 feet (45 metres) above sea level crossed by tributaries of the River Blyth. These streams form reasonably deep valleys that the "B" roads follow, meaning that virtually every junction of any substance on the ride involves a short steep uphill and downhill.

There are few tourist attractions on the ride, although there are several notable churches. Saint Mary's at Huntingfield with its marvellous 19th century painted ceiling is one of the great folk art curiosities of the region. The Vicar's wife apparently painted the ceiling by lying on top of scaffolding. This will strike a chord with the present day spouses of rural clergy who are forced to undertake many and varied support roles!

The absence of tourist honeypots makes this an excellent summer ride as most motoring visitors keep to the coast or bigger towns.

What to Expect

This 19-mile ride is all on good tarmac roads, so it is a fine all year round route. Much of the ride is on quiet minor roads with short sections on relatively little-used "B" roads. However, a short section of the A1120 is included (the excellent Sustrans map gives an alternative diversion but this involves breaking the author's rather dogmatic rule of never covering the same piece of road twice in a ride). The "A" road is only followed for a quarter of a mile but it does carry lorries and care is needed.

The ride gets a 'level three' difficulty rating, mainly because of its length but also due to occasional short, sharp climbs and the use of the A1120 in Peasenhall.

There are several shops in Peasenhall (Emmetts Store is particularly recommended for its smoked delicacies), and pubs on the ride in Sibton and a short distance off route in Huntingfield and Wissett.

Byways Cycles at Priory Farm, Darsham (01728 668764) offers cycle hire and sales as well as repairs. There is also another bike shop off the route in Halesworth called O'Neills of a vintage and style no longer seen in the Home Counties; this is truly in a time warp.

Getting Started

Starting Point: The Street, Peasenhall – OS Grid Reference TM357693.

The ride starts from The Street in Peasenhall where there is on-street parking. Beware, however, when unloading children, dogs and bikes, as this is the A1120.

Peasenhall is on the National Cycle Network, meaning that this ride is ideally approached by bike. It can be linked to Route 11 (the Godric Way) by a three-mile section of back roads from St Margaret South Eltham through Rumburgh to Wissett.

For a change rail access is good. The station at Halesworth is just one and a half miles off the route, and the connecting section is part of the National Cycle Network.

The Route

From the starting point ride west along the A1120 before carefully taking the right turn **(1)** in the direction signposted to Heveningham and Harleston.

This road climbs up away from Peasenhall; follow the signposts to Heveningham and Harleston climbing past an electricity sub-station on the right. Immediately after there is a steep downhill to a stream crossing, and then another climb onto the Roman Road, which leads towards Heveningham. The Roman Road runs dead straight for 1¾ miles past a poultry farm, then orchards on the right, with the church in Heveningham coming into view in a dip.

The road dips down to a T-junction with the B1117. Take a right **(2)** signposted to Heveningham, Walpole and Halesworth. After a couple of hundred yards on the B1117 take the left turn signposted to Huntingfield, Linstead and Harleston with Heveningham church straight ahead. The road drops sharply downhill, follow it round to the right **(3)** in the direction signposted to Huntingfield, Linstead and Rumburgh as you leave this village.

The road climbs steeply away from the village in the direction of Linstead with a pig farm on the right. Continue straight through this open, upland agricultural area and go straight across the crossroads. A detour to the right here will take those already tiring to a pub in Huntingfield.

Across the fields to the right can be seen Heveningham Hall, a grand Palladian house set in magnificent grounds landscaped by "Capability

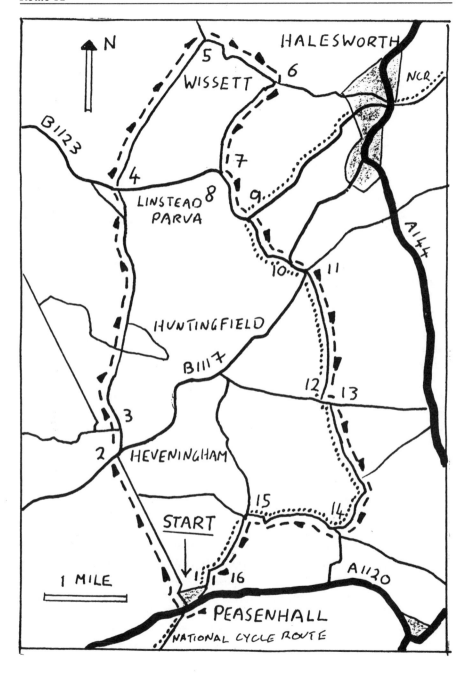

N

HALESWORTH

WISSETT

NCR

B1123

5

6

4

7

LINSTEAD
PARVA

8

9

10

11

A144

HUNTINGFIELD

B1117

12 13

3

2

HEVENINGHAM

15

14

START

1 MILE

1

16

A1120

PEASENHALL

NATIONAL CYCLE ROUTE

Brown". The road then drops down into the village of Huntingfield with the church of Saint Mary's on your right, with the Manor House on the other bank of the River Blythe

Although remnants from as early as the 10th century can be seen on the site, the main interest in St Mary's church is the magnificent hammer beam roof, and in particular the carved angels and brilliantly painted woodwork. The paintwork dates from the 1860s and is a magnificent example of folk art. The splendid roof can be illuminated to order by putting a £1 coin in a meter; it is money well spent.

Leaving the church behind the road climbs back up on to the plateau passing Molecatchers Cottage on your left, then going straight ahead across the crossroads in the direction signposted to Linstead Parva and Halesworth.

Two miles from Huntingfield church, bear right just after Linstead House on your right. Follow the road to the right ignoring the left turn, there is a sharp downhill past 30mph signs to a staggered crossroads.

On the right of this junction is St Margaret's church, Linstead. This pretty church was probably built early in the 12th century. There were extensive changes in the 15th century when most of the windows were enlarged and again in the late 19th century when many fittings were incorporated from the abandoned church of St Peter's in the village.

At the staggered crossroads (4) go straight ahead (slightly to the right) in the direction signposted to Rumburgh. This sunken lane again climbs back onto the plateau with its productive agricultural land. Go straight past Town Farm and the orchards before dropping and climbing again to a T-junction.

Go right at this T-junction (5) in the direction signposted to Wissett and Halesworth to begin the return journey back towards Peasenhall. After half a mile road enters the village of Wissett with the church of St Andrew on the right. A short distance past the church is the Plough, which makes an excellent mid-point lunch stop.

St Andrew's church is based on Saxon construction, and its distinctive round tower probably dates from around 900AD, with the thickness of the walls confirming that it is pre-Conquest. This design of round tower is common in Norfolk and Suffolk with around 200 examples, but rare outside these counties. Another striking feature is the fine 15th century font of the type often found in east Suffolk and Norfolk. The tower contains six bells, one of which was cast in Bristol between 1350 and 1380 and is one of the oldest in Suffolk.

The route takes the right turn before the church **(6)** called Lodge Lane and signposted to Chediston and Linstead. The road zigzags as it climbs away from the church and the village, and passes several farms before dropping down into Chediston with a large pond on the right and reaching a T-junction.

At this T-junction **(7)** turn left signposted to Linstead and Halesworth and drop down through the village to reach the B1123 at a junction. At this T-junction **(8)** take the left signposted to Halesworth and continue for three-quarters of a mile before taking the right turn **(9)** signposted to Cookley and Walpole by the white sign saying Cookley Grange.

The road climbs and bears left past Rockstone Manor before sweeping downhill to a T-junction with the B1117. At this point the route joins the National Cycle Network and follows it all the way back to Peasenhall, so Sustrans excellent map can be used as a supplementary guide.

At this junction **(10)** turn right signposted to Walpole, Stradbroke and Eye. Follow the B1117 for just a quarter of a mile until it turns right. Take the second turning on the left **(11)** at the bend signposted to Bramfield and Yoxford.

This lane again climbs up away from the "B" road passing the stump of a windmill on the left and after a mile reaches a T-junction. At this T-junction **(12)** take the left signposted to Bramfield and Yoxford and after 100 yards, take the right turn **(13)** signposted to Yoxford. The impressive house that can be seen on the left through the trees is Bramfield House, now a school.

The route once again winds across the agricultural plateau passing Earlsway Farm on the right. Continue straight ahead on this road ignoring the left turn to Bramfield as it twists and turns through farms for almost two miles to another T-junction. Go right at this junction **(14)** signposted to Heveningham and Laxfield, and follow the road in the direction of Heveningham through Sibton Green. Go past High House Farm towards the crossroads with the water tower on the edge of Lodge Wood, which has been visible for much of the ride, now close by on the left.

When you reach the crossroads at the main road turn left **(15)** in the direction signposted to Peasenhall, Yoxford and Framlingham. The road drops down into Sibton and reaches the White Horse Pub. Bear left after this and cross the narrow bridge, and follow the road as it bears right to bring you to the A1120 in Peasenhall. Carefully turn right **(16)** out on to the "A" road, and you are back to the starting point of the ride.

Route 13
Framlingham to Blaxhall

Distance: 31 miles

Difficulty Level: 3

Map: OS Landranger 156 – Saxmundham

Setting the Scene

This magnificent ride should be sub-titled the "mini Loire tour" as it offers a superb castle and renown vineyards complete with wine tasting, without the hassle of travelling hundreds of miles overseas.

The starting point for the ride is the delightful Suffolk town of Framlingham whose delights match with ease those of comparable French "villes". Framlingham has everything a civilised small town should have, an immaculate castle, excellent shops including an outstanding bookshop, and a good choice of eating (and drinking) places.

The high spot of the town both topographically and aesthetically is the Castle. Built from limestone imported from Northamptonshire by boat, Framlingham Castle has remained virtually intact as it only came under siege once (in 1215).

The continental feel introduced by a castle and sleepy river is enhanced by the local vineyards, which benefit from the areas good soils and kind climate. Two of the leading wineries are on the ride, giving an opportunity for French (or Nappa Valley?) style tastings *en route*.

No one should be misled into thinking that these vineyards are but pale imitations of their continental cousins. In fact far from it, as the best vine stock and production techniques are used to produce high quality wines that do not need to hide behind their East Anglian origins.

Bruisyard vineyard cultivates 10 acres containing 13 000 Muller Thurgau vines, with production dating back 25 years. Shawsgate vineyard, which is literally a short cycle ride away, cultivates 17 acres making it one of the largest in the region. Here again Muller Thurgau grapes, originating from the Palatinate region of Germany, have been supplemented by other varieties to produce award winning white and more recently rose wines. Shawsgate is an example of the major investment in viticulture in the region, as instanced by the latest stainless steel winemaking equipment.

The ride has much else to offer. Picture postcard cottages and water mills, abundant wildlife, and an optional detour to Snape and on to the estuary of the River Alde.

What to Expect

The route is a triangle with a flat base. The two upward-pointing sides are the "inland" and "coastal" routes of Sustrans' excellent National Cycle Network, which divides at the apex at Bruisyard (also noted for its vineyard). The flat base linking the other two sides is a Sustrans "link Route".

This all means that two-thirds of the 31 miles are on the designated

National Cycle Network, and the balance is on approved linking roads. The result is excellent riding with just one road level-crossing of an "A" road, plus limited riding on quiet "B" roads.

Adding to the appeal of the ride is the fact that the two parts using the National Cycle Network also form part of the Suffolk Coastal Cycle Route which is clearly waymarked, although this does make the unsignposted link between Dallington and Blaxhall irritatingly difficult to follow. The full Suffolk Coastal Cycle

Route is 75 miles. A full map giving additional information is available from Suffolk Connexions, 36-38 St Helen's Street, Ipswich IP4 2JZ.

The entire ride is on reasonable quality metalled roads, although farm vehicles and rain run-off can make these sandy or muddy depending on the weather.

A difficulty level 3 (out of a maximum of 4) is awarded mostly due to the length and some mild gradients. Although absolutely delightful, riding the route can be a bit "fiddly" due to the numerous turnings and crossroads, particularly on the central section which does not benefit from waymarkings.

For a change, refreshment stops and shops are not problems. In fact, two vineyards in the last four miles of riding offer a powerful incentive to reach the end of the ride!

Getting Started

Starting Point: Elms Car Park, Framlingham – OS Grid Ref. TM282638.

The starting point of the ride is highly convenient for cyclists using the Hull to Harwich route to combine a number of routes as it actually lies on the National Cycle Network. Other rides in this book can easily be accessed by bike, the closest starting at Peasenhall just two and a half miles to the north of Bruisyard.

A railway station also lies on the ride at Wickham Market with connections to Ipswich and Norwich.

For car users, Framlingham lies between the A12 trunk road and the A1120.

The Route

From the starting point in Elms Car Park in Framlingham turn left into New Road and ride down to the junction at the bottom **(1)**.

At this T-junction, you will see the first of many green and yellow Suffolk Coastal Cycle Route signs, which will be followed for a considerable part of the ride.

Follow the signs, turn right at the bottom of New Road into Bridge Street, and immediately turn right again at the next T-junction and cycle up the hill past the White Horse Pub on the left.

This main road is the B1119. After just 100 yards, turn left following the

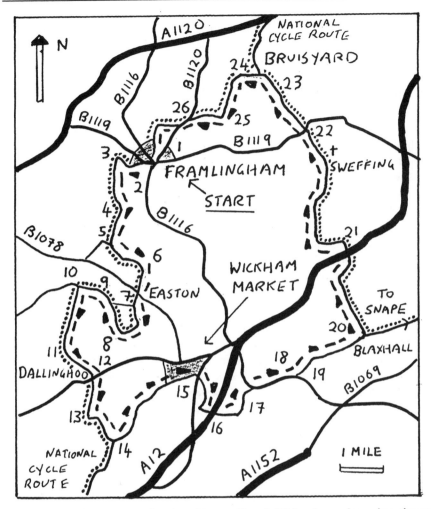

Suffolk Coastal Route sign into Vyces Road. Ride along dropping down-hill to the left to reach another T-junction with a minor road.

Turn right here **(2)** again following the Suffolk Coastal Route sign. This pleasant lane with a stream on the right and bank on the left takes a sharp right turn and then climbs uphill.

At the top of this short, sharp hill take the left turn off the road **(3)**. The turning is not signposted but is again marked with a Suffolk Coastal Route sign.

Stay straight ahead on this road as it passes through a small farm and then drops downhill through rolling landscape. This is not the dead flat open landscape usually associated with East Anglia, but gentle green valleys cutting into the agricultural uplands.

After a mile at the T-junction with a busier road, turn right at the hamlet of Lampard Brook. Again, there is a Suffolk Coastal Route arrow but no signpost **(4)**. This road climbs back up on to the more exposed upland.

After another mile, the road turns sharp right in the direction of Kettleburgh. Do not follow the road round to the right but instead take the left turn off at the bend in the direction indicated by a Suffolk Coastal Route arrow and signposted to Easton and Wickham Market **(5)**.

This minor road drops downhill to reach yet another T-junction **(6)**. Turn right again following the Suffolk Coastal Route sign and the signpost to Easton.

A straight section of a mile passes Easton Park on the left, and then enters the village of Easton with impressive properties on both sides of the road.

Ride through the village and on the other side as the main road bears left turn off right following the Suffolk Coastal Route arrow in the direction signposted to Leatheringham and Monewden **(7)**.

As you ride away from the junction look to the right at the unusual circular thatched cottage. Almost immediately turn left off this road again following the Suffolk Coastal Route arrow and the signposts for Leatheringham, Woodbridge and Watermill. The road crosses the River Deben on a small bridge, and then passes Leatheringham Watermill and Gardens on the right, which are occasionally open to the public.

After passing Leatheringham Hall on the right the road climbs to the village of Leatheringham and reaches a T-junction **(8)**. Go right here following the Suffolk Coastal Route arrow and the signposts to Hoo, Kettleburgh and Monewden.

It is difficult to imagine a more enticing English country scene with beautifully preserved cottages with their gardens reaching down to the river. The road follows the Deben for a short distance before reaching another T-junction **(9)**. Go left following the Suffolk Coastal Route arrow and signposts to Hoo Green and Monewden.

After three-quarters of a mile, turn left at the next T-junction again in the direction of the Suffolk Coastal Route arrow and the signpost to Monewden, Charsfield and Woodbridge **(10)**.

Ride straight ahead for a mile and a quarter in the village of Charsfield. Immediately after passing the church of St Peter, Charsfield, take the left turn off the main road **(11)**. This turn is marked with a Suffolk Coastal Route arrow and is signposted to Dallinghoo, Melton and Bridge.

Shortly after leaving the village, the B1078 is reached. Turn left out on to the "B" road following the Suffolk Coastal Route and the signpost to Bredfield and Wickham Market **(12)**. After 100 yards, turn right off the B1078 immediately after the petrol station following the Suffolk Coastal Route sign. Straight after turning off the main road, there is another T-junction. Turn left and almost immediately right down a small side road marked with a Suffolk Coastal Route arrow. Follow this little lane as it winds into the village of Dallinghoo past the church of St Mary on the left.

Beyond the church is a T-junction **(13)**, take a right following the Suffolk Coastal Route arrow and the signpost to Bredfield and Woodbridge. Ride out of Dallinghoo in the direction of Bredfield with the spire in Wickham Market briefly visible on the left.

A short distance after this junction turn left in the direction signposted Wickham Market and Pettistree **(14)**. At this junction the rides leaves the waymarked Suffolk Coastal Route and there are no signs at this turning or for the next eight miles. Take care not to miss this turning, it is immediately next to the Hall and opposite a rather attractive pond with bulrushes.

After taking this turn follow the winding road towards Wickham Market with the spire of the church visible as you ride in towards the town. This road takes you in through the outskirts of Wickham Market past the Primary School on the left before reaching the Square in the Town Centre. Wickham Market is an attractive small town with a range of shops, pubs and cafes plus public toilets in the central square. The Tea Pot tearoom on the right serves morning and afternoon tea, coffee and a selection of light and hot lunches.

At the Square turn right which takes you to the B1438. Turn right out on to the "B" road in the direction of Woodbridge **(15)**. After a short distance on the B1438, turn off left into Chapel Lane by the War Memorial; this turning has no signposts other than one saying "Library".

Follow Chapel Lane out though a residential area into open countryside, and stay on this narrow lane as it heads towards the roar of the A12. The road runs parallel to the A12 for a short distance and reaches a T-junction **(16)**. Turn left and cross the busy A12 high above it on a bridge.

Keep straight ahead from this bridge passing the gates to the Hall on the right, and crossing the River Denon twice. Ash Abbey is on the right just after the second river crossing beyond the magnificent Mill House, which can be seen from the road.

Shortly after Mill House, the road reaches a T-junction adjacent to a railway bridge. Go left at this junction (17), then after a short distance take an unmarked right at the next junction opposite the entrance to Quill Farm and the public footpath.

After a quarter of a mile, this brings you through a built-up area to a T-junction with the B1078. Turn right here (18) onto the main road in the direction signposted to Tunstall and Orford, riding past Wickham Market Station on the right and up over the railway bridge.

Stay on the B1078 for a mile in the direction of Orford until reaching a sharp right turn in the road (19). At this bend take the left turn off the main road in the direction signposted to Blaxhall, Snape and Youth Hostel.

Stay on this road as it takes a sharp right turn, and follow it for almost two miles in the direction of Blaxhall. Before entering the village, take the left turn signposted to Little Glenham (20). At this point, the ride rejoins the Suffolk Coastal Route with its excellent signing. However, at the time of researching, the one pointing towards Little Glenham at this junction was missing. An optional detour can be made here by staying straight ahead and riding a mile and a half to the famous concert Hall at Snape Maltings, and then on to the village of Snape itself.

Follow the signs in the direction of Little Glenham, crossing an automated level crossing and bridge over a stream in the direction of Stratford and Saxmundham.

This road reaches the busy A12 and should be crossed with extreme caution to the tarmac cycle path that is part of the admirable National Cycle Network development (21). Cycle along the path and turn left into the side turning and away from the bustle of the trunk route.

After a short climb take the left turn marked by the Suffolk Coastal Route arrow. The next nine miles are some of the most enjoyable on the Hull to Harwich National Cycle Network. The scenery is delightful, the route is almost traffic-free and clearly signed, and the cyclist is simply left thanking Sustrans for this marvellous facility.

After a mile and a half this very quiet road reaches a crossroads, go straight ahead in the direction of Sweffling and Rendham. A mile further turn left at the T-junction following the Suffolk Coastal Route arrow towards Cranford and Badingham.

Stay on this road in the direction of Dennington and Laxfield and into the village of Sweffling. Cycle through the village past the parish church of St Mary, following the road as it drops down to a crossroads with the B1119 at the White Horse Inn **(22)**.

Go straight across the "B" road in the direction of the Suffolk Coastal Route arrow in the direction of Peasenhall and Walpole. After crossing the River Alde the road goes left and is signposted to Bruisyard Vineyard **(23)**. After 100 yards, take the turning off to the left by the village sign in the direction of the Suffolk Coastal Route arrow and signposted towards Badingham, Laxfield and Bruisyard church and vineyard.

Just past this junction the magnificent Bruisyard Hall is set back from the road on the right-hand side. As the road drops down after the Hall take the left turn marked with a Suffolk Coastal Route arrow and signposted to Bruisyard Vineyard.

After crossing a gentle ford on the right-hand side is the rather extraordinary sight, for Suffolk, of an expanse of beautifully tended and pruned vines. In addition to the vineyard, Bruisyard has a winery, herb and water gardens – check opening times by phoning Badingham 281.

After the vineyard and another stream crossing, go right at the T-junction following the Suffolk Coastal Route arrow **(24)**. Almost immediately, turn left following the signs in the direction to Cranford.

The road climbs up out of the valley and it is good to see signs here saying that the verge is a protected roadside nature reserve.

At Red House Farm, Cranford, a T-junction is reached. Go right here following the Suffolk Coastal Route arrow **(25)**. After a mile of cycling along this straight, open and sometimes windy road, the B1120 is reached **(26)**.

Turn left here following the Suffolk coastal Route arrow in the direction of Framlingham and Wickham Market. Shortly after joining the main road on the right-hand side is another vineyard, Shawsgate, producing fine quality English wines.

Shortly after passing the vineyard leave the "B" road by turning right at the Suffolk Coastal Route arrow into the byroad. The road drops down with a farm straight ahead, follow the road as it turns sharp left clearly marked with an arrow.

It is then downhill all the way back into Framlingham passing through the immaculately kept college grounds with a fine view of the castle on the left. As the road enters Framlingham the starting point of the route is on the left in the Elms Car Park.

Route 14
Rutland Water

Distance: 17 or 25 miles

Difficulty Level: 2 to 3

Map: OS Landranger 141 – Kettering and Corby

Setting the Scene

Arguably Rutland Water lies on the western edge of the Midlands rather than the eastern side of East Anglia, with Cambridgeshire starting some 12 miles to the east. However, four good reasons prompt its inclusion in this volume. First Rutland Water is an exemplary example of the development of a leisure resource from an economic necessity – in this case a man-made reservoir. Secondly the land managers are Anglian Water who supply most of the area covered in this book, and thirdly it is located conveniently close to three of the main access routes into East Anglia (A1, A47 and A14). Finally Rutland Water can offer, what very few other routes in this book can, hills. Although we are not talking about Lake District type elevations the path that circumnavigates the Water offers interesting climbs and vantage points across this superb 3100-acre stretch of inland water.

Anglian Water manages Grafham Water (Route 16), Alton Water near Ipswich, and Pitsford north of Northampton, all of which offer cycling facilities.

Rutland Water is the largest man-made lake in Western Europe, and was formed as a water supply to East Anglia. In conjunction with its present managers Anglian Water, a first class network of leisure facilities has been created around the lake including a Water Sports facility, Butterfly and Aquatic Centre, Drought Garden and Museum.

A purpose constructed cycle path surrounds the lake, using some sections of road as links. There are numerous refreshment points and good toilet facilities. Cycle Hire is available at Whitwell and Normanton during the season.

Rutland Water is really a gem, in the right weather and out of the summer peak season it is a very appealing ride for the leisure cyclists wanting to venture off tarmac without scaling the heights of the Peak or Lake District. The views across the lake with hundreds of sailing boats are the more remarkable for being within easy reach of London, Birmingham and other urban areas. But the area can get crowded and the excellent bike trail is a strictly multi-user path, so this is not a ride for "hammer-head" mountain-bikers, a species which inevitably must be contained on closed riding areas if access problems of Californian proportions are to be avoided in the UK.

What to Expect

For the recreational cyclist the main attraction is the cycle path around Rutland Water. The path makes a 17-mile circuit of the lake, with an optional 8-mile loop around the picturesque Hambleton Peninsula.

Sections around the north side car parks of Whitwell and Empingham suit family cyclists, and provide delightful views of the lake, coupled with a full range of amenities including an Adventure Playground at Empingham. Road and children's bikes are suitable for this area, however the Hambleton Peninsula loop in particular requires a mountain bike. There are some steeper gradients around Barnsdale Park, and children and beginners are best to keep to Whitwell, Empingham and the eastern end.

The track used by bikes is a multi-user path shared with walkers, and due care must be exercised. Rutland Water is a major tourist attraction and can get very busy in the summer. As with many areas in East Anglia a visit out of the peak season makes a lot of sense for the more serious cyclists. Beware however the car parks close at dusk in the winter, so pace your ride to arrive back at your car with time in hand.

Although 100 per cent rideable by a reasonably competent mountain biker, sections of the route are unsuitable for the more casual cyclist. The surface varies from tarmac to metalled paths and bare earth in places, and there are some sizeable loose stones. Although rideable all year, the path gets wet and boggy for short stretches, and the rough mettalled surface can become slippery.

A full circuit of the lake is for the more experienced cyclist – the circuitous nature of the route means there are no short cuts back to the start (bar swimming!) if a rider tires. As well as variable surfaces and gradients there are road sections on the southern side. Allow a full day for a complete circuit at a leisurely pace including Hambleton, although this can be shortened by seven miles by omitting the peninsula loop.

The Hambleton Peninsula offers the best cycling for suitably equipped riders, on a quiet day the lakeside sections resemble a mini-Scotland or Austria. Hambleton Hall on the peninsula, now a hotel, was host to Noel Coward when he wrote "Blyth Spirit".

A sensible option to avoid having to ride a full circuit is to park in the Barnsdale Car Park proceed west and ride the Hambleton loop, and then retrace the route back to Barnsdale making an attractive twelve-mile ride. The peninsula loop uses a one way system that keeps cycle traffic on the twisty lake side paths moving in the same direction.

The cycle path includes tarmac and road sections. West of Barnsdale a tarmac path runs parallel to the busy A606 and the A6003. The outward route of the Hambledon Peninsula route uses a straight, quiet and somewhat boring tarmac road, while west of Manton there are several miles on an unclassified through road which carries traffic to access points on the south side of the lake, this road can be busy at weekends.

Getting Started

Rutland Water is east of Oakham between the A606 and A6003. Access from the A1 is via the A606 exit. There are railway stations at Stamford and Oakham both of which are close to the lake, albeit via very busy "A" roads.

There are four official car parks around the Water with good amenities. At the time of writing a £1 daily car park charge applies, transferable between parks. The three car parks off the A606 offer the best cycling options. Short leisure rides can be made between Whitwell and Eppingham, with an Adventure Playground and Butterfly Centre at the latter.

The Route

The bike path is clearly waymarked so, as with similar routes in this book, detailed directions are not given. Instead, this section will concentrate on general orientation and route options.

The basic decision at this venue is whether to make a full circuit of the lake, or instead opt for an "out and back" route. A full circuit also offers the option of including, or bypassing the Hambleton Peninsula, although it is strongly recommended to include this if at all possible as it offers some of the most rewarding riding in the area.

A full circuit of Rutland Water including the Peninsula is 23 miles with

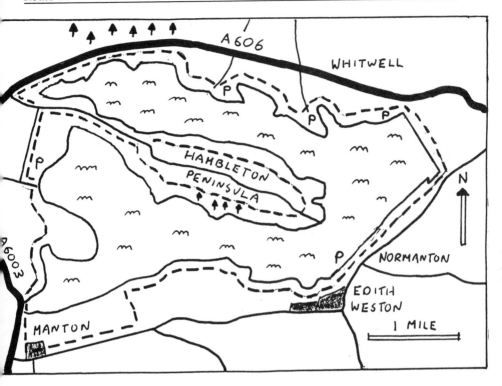

some (by East Anglian standards!) climbing, and is really suited to more experienced cyclists riding mountain bikes. For the full tour it is best to park in the Whitwell car park (where cycle hire is available in season) and head west towards Barnsdale for an anti-clockwise lap. This route has the advantage of getting the tarmac and hilly bits (and easterly headwind) over in the first half of the ride, leaving a more leisurely ride home from Normanton onwards, with the tarmac sections either side of the Hambleton Peninsula and on the entry to the Peninsula itself. The home section from Normanton on an anti-clockwise lap is almost flat with an open section before Empingham across the dyke that forming the eastern end of the lake.

If the chosen option is a full circuit without the Hambleton Peninsula loop the route follow the clearly marked turning to Egleton instead of going to Hambleton.

The "strenuous but shorter" option for mountain bikes is to park in the Barnsdale car park and head west to the Hambleton Peninsula, make this loop and then return back in the reverse direction to Barnsdale.

For more relaxed riding the Empingham car park with its Adventure Playground is the best base. A short ride can be taken west to Whitwell and back, or a longer (eight relatively flat miles) can be taken by heading clock-wise to Normanton and back. Both rides give an excellent flavour of the area without becoming over ambitious. The ride to Normanton allows a visit to the church and Water Museum at the Leisure Area giving a good picture of the local history of the area now covered by Rutland Water. It is also worth mentioning the novel drought garden created by Anglian Water at the Barnsdale Leisure Centre. This project shows a garden created without any watering additional to natural rainfall, a topical subject as global warming continues to change our weather patterns.

Route 15
Ely to Ten-Mile Bank

Distance: 36 miles

Difficulty Level: 4

Map: OS Landranger 143 – Ely and Wisbech

Setting the Scene

For once that overworked word "unique" can be correctly used to de-scribe this ride which explores the Fenlands, north of Ely. The ride crosses a landscape quite unlike anything found elsewhere in the British Isles. This is totally flat terrain with panoramic skyscapes, and dead straight waterways, with often the road and isolated houses below the water level.

The ride follows a triangular route, along the Great Ouse to a northern apex, then returning south parallel to the Hundred Foot Washes before running west to east between the two waterways to return to the starting point at Ely.

The first section follows the banks of the Great Ouse in ten miles of al-most uninterrupted level cycling, while the return leg follows the old Bed-ford River, now a man-made drainage channel, for another dead straight five miles.

The Fens to the north of Ely have been reclaimed from wetlands by re-peated efforts starting in Roman and Anglo Saxon times. In the early 17th century a Dutch engineer, Cornelius Vermuyden, was responsible for draining the remaining wetlands to establish the geography we are now familiar with.

Rich black alluvial soils make this a very productive agricultural area, and farming dominates the landscape away from Ely. Farms and cot-tages for farm workers dot this sparsely populated area with a climate that alternates between strong winds and damp mists. Legends of sor-cery and web-footed inhabitants date back to medieval times when the bleak area comprised small islands separated by yet to be drained chan-nels.

The high spot of the Fens, both spiritually and geographically, is the Isle of Ely. Although today the description Isle refers to the city's position alongside the Great Ouse river; the name Ely is literally derived from Eel Island.

The glory of Ely, not to mention the Fens and East Anglia is the great Cathedral. This magnificent building dates from Norman times but its aesthetic impact dates from the 14th century. At this time, work on the marvellous Lady Chapel caused the great central Norman tower to collapse, demolishing the Norman choir at the same time. Following this disaster, Alan of Walsingham built the mighty octagon in its place, and it is this magnificent structure crowned by a wooden lantern that can be seen as a landmark from many points on the ride.

Fittingly the ride starts and finishes outside the superb west front of the cathedral, and there is little excuse for even the most church shy cyclist to avoid enjoying one of the architectural wonders of the British Isle. Ely Cathedral is a "must see". This truly unique route, with its miles of uninterrupted cycling across countryside reclaimed relatively recently from nature, is similarly a "must" ride for the more experienced cyclist.

Ten Mile Bank

What to Expect

Throughout this book every effort has been made to avoid using "A" roads for rides, and to minimise the use of "B" roads. Unfortunately roads are a scarce resource in the Fens as they require laborious building on raised embankments. For this reason it proved to be impossible to make a complete route including the very attractive riding country north of Ely without using two short stretches of "A" roads. Rather than dogmatically exclude the route because of this it is included with the caution that a total of one and a quarter miles of not very busy "A" roads are used.

This ride is rated at the highest difficulty level of four for a combination of reasons. The use of "A" roads requires caution and experience, as does the relatively short stretch through Ely. At 36 miles this is one of the longest routes in the book, and while still being considerably less than a day's cycling it can be both physically and psychologically punishing in poor and in particularly windy weather. There is very little in the way of either shelter or refreshments on the first 27 miles of this ride.

The great majority of the ride is on good metalled roads and there are no off-road sections. However, the section from the Hundred Foot Washes to Little Downham is on a crazed road surface that will do little for lightweight racing wheels, so sturdy running gear is recommended.

Ely has a full range of shops and restaurants, but after leaving this fine city there are few other amenities. The Windmill at Ten Mile Bank, at the northern point of the ride, offers refreshments and is open all day at weekends. Nevertheless, from there it is a very long haul to Little Downham for the next shops and refreshments.

Getting Started

Starting Point: Ely Cathedral – OS Grid Ref. TL541802.

Ely is blessed with good railway connections, and the station is only a short distance from the start of the ride. Road access is excellent via the A10 or A142. Long term pay and display parking is available off Fore Hill.

The Sustrans National Cycle Network passes to the north and can be accessed from St John's Fen End in a 14-mile ride via Downham Market.

This ride on the north-eastern extremity of those covered in this book, and is some distance from other routes, Route 9 (Castle Acre and Litcham is the closest).

The Route

The ride starts from outside the magnificent west entrance to Ely Cathedral **(1)**. Take the one way road that runs in front of the Cathedral and cycle along it in the direction signposted to the Station and Stuntney.

The road drops downhill, take the left turn into Forehill . As the road starts to bear left take the right turn signposted to The Maltings and River, then almost immediately turn left again into Lisle Street. Cycle straight up Lisle Lane past the big Post Office depot on your right. Follow the road as it climbs uphill and bears left before coming to a T-junction with the B1382.

At this T-junction **(2)** turn right onto the B1382 in the direction signposted to Pickwillow. Cycle straight ahead through the outskirts of Ely, first passing a new housing development on the left, then dropping down across a railway bridge followed by two level crossings. Just after the second level crossing the road crosses the river. Immediately after this bridge take the left turn **(3)** signposted to Littleport.

The ride now follows the Great Ouse in a dead straight line through a classic flat landscape with fields stretching to the horizon on the right, and the towering man-made river embankment on the left. Keep straight ahead on this road ignoring the left turn across the bridge at Sandhill giving access to Littleport. However, if rejuvenation is required at this early stage of the ride the Black Swan Pub is just the other side of the bridge.

Stay straight ahead ignoring the left turn across the bridge and continue in the direction signposted to Mildenhall, Downham Market and Southery until the roundabout at the junction with the A1101 is reached.

At this roundabout go carefully left **(4)** out onto the A1101 in the direction signposted to London, Ely, Wisbech and Littleport. Cross the river bridge and immediately turn right off the "A" road into the side road signposted to Black Horse Drove. This short section of "A" road can easily be walked if required.

The road turning right off the A101 is Ten Mile Bank, and after precisely ten miles of following the towering riverbank the village of Ten Mile Bank is reached. (Ignore the left turn into Black Horse Drove.)

These are ten miles of unique cycling, almost dead straight without any gradient at all, with astonishing vistas of field and sky. Fortunately the last section of the ride runs atop the riverbank giving superb views along the Great Ouse.

In the village of Ten Mile Bank take the left turn **(5)** signposted to Welney. The Windmill Pub just across the bridge on the right makes a

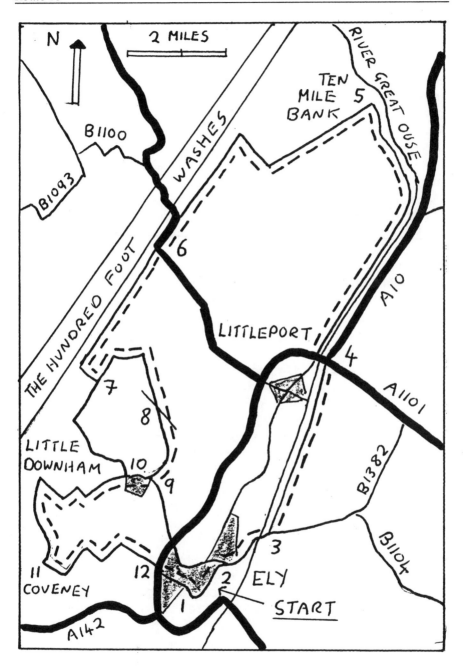

convenient lunch stop; there are no more shops or pubs for the next 17 miles!

After taking the left turn, cycle out of Ten Mile Bank past the Primary School on your left, into open country again. This road is dead straight for three miles, crossing an automatic level crossing and then turning sharp right before reaching The Hundred Foot Marsh, and turning south to follow the course of the Old Bedford River in another dead straight line for more than five miles.

This road passes the Wild Fowl Trust Visitors Centre before joining the A1001 adjacent to the suspension bridge across The Hundred Foot Marsh. Carefully join the "A" road **(6)** and continue straight ahead following the river embankment. Just after the sign for the boundary between Norfolk and Cambridgeshire the "A" road turns sharp left away from the river. Do not follow the main road but instead take the right turn onto the minor road, which continues to follow the river and is signposted to Little Downham and Pymoor.

The minor road is the B1411 although there are no identifying signs at this point. This road continues straight ahead for another two and a half miles with only the intriguingly named Four Balls Farm on the left providing a little light relief.

Towards the end of this straight section the road passes the Hundred Foot Pumping Station which started life in 1756 as a windmill, before being upgraded in 1830 to steam power and finally in 1926 to oil power. The pumping station can remove 200 tonnes of water a minute from the surrounding land, which is under constant threat of being submerged again. (In fact shortly after the author completed the ride this whole area was submerged in some of the worst flooding for decades.)

Shortly after this pumping station the road passes under a railway bridge and then leaves the river in a sharp left turn. After a quarter of a mile the main road turns sharp right, at this bend take the left turn off the B1411 into the single-track road signposted to Pymoor Sidings **(7)**.

Follow this single-track road straight ahead and under the railway, then keep on it as it turns right over a bridge crossing a drainage channel. Stay straight ahead ignoring the signpost for the public byway on the right. Stay on the metalled but bumpy road as it winds through a multitude of farm buildings ignoring the left turn into Fourth Drove.

Stay on the road as it crosses the railway at an automatic level crossing before reaching a T-junction. **(8)** Go left at this T-junction which has no signpost. If the weather is unkind there is a convenient covered bus shelter complete with seat along on the left suitable for a short break.

Keep on the main road ignoring the various turnings on the left as it enters the mysteriously named hamlet of California (birthplace of mountain biking?) and becomes Layne Lane. Follow this road through the residential area to the T-junction with the B1411.

(9) Turn right out on to the B1411 in the direction signposted to Pymoor and Welney and ride into the village of Little Downham, with the parish church of St Leonard on the right. Downham has a range of shops with a general store and post office on the left, and at the end of the village on the right is the Plough Pub dating from 1799.

Stay on the "B" road as it leaves the village **(10)**. When the main road turns sharp right leave it going straight ahead onto a minor road signposted to Coveney and Wardyhill. On your left are views across the fields to Ely Cathedral.

Follow this good secondary road as it snakes through various farms and cottages to reach Coveney. Cycle into the village past the pretty church of St Peter's on the right. Immediately after the old village school, with its bell tower, **(11)** take the left turn signposted to Ely.

Ely is now clearly visible ahead and the road follows a typical course of straights interspersed by right angle bends as it crosses open farm land towards the City.

At the outskirts of Ely this road reaches the busy A10. Cross straight over with great care **(12)** into West Fen Road and follow this into the city to reach a T-junction. Go right at this junction, then at the crossroads immediately afterwards cross straight over this busy road into the one way street opposite.

This one way street passes the parish church of St Mary the Virgin with a magnificent view of the cathedral ahead. The street bears sharp right, at this point dismount and walk across Palace Green to arrive back at the west entrance to the cathedral, and the starting point of the ride.

Route 16
Grafham Water

Distance: 10 miles

Difficulty Level: 2

Map: OS Landranger 153 – Bedford and Huntingdon

Setting the Scene

Like Ride 14 – Rutland Water – this highly recommended route follows a cycle path around one of Anglia Water's man-made reservoirs. A dam at the east end, which was completed in 1964 from waterproof clay, forms the lake. The dam is 1700 metres long, 24 metres high and 300 metres thick. 1.7 million cubic metres of materials were used to build it and it holds back 13 million gallons of water pumped from the nearby river, Great Ouse (which also features in ride 15 around Ely). The water travels six kilometres through steel pipes from the pumping station at Offord, passing under the A1 trunk road to the reservoir with a maximum daily flow of 92 million gallons a day.

The 1500-acre park was opened in 1966 with facilities for sailing and fishing, and following major landscaping in 1991 the cycle path and cycle hire facilities were introduced. There are now a full range of amenities including car parking (pay and display), a well-stocked bike shop, toilets, café and exhibition centre. The whole ride is on the purpose-built bike path except for a short road section through the villages of Perry and Grafham.

Grafham Water is really a quite delightful place for relaxed family cycling and has become something of a Mecca for cyclists. The lake is set in beautiful countryside and the cycle path offers unique views across the water.

Because of its attractions the area can become quite crowded and busy at summer weekends. The facilities including cycle hire are open all year round so an out of season visit is worth considering.

What to Expect

The bike path has a durable gravel surface that should be rideable in all but the most extreme weather conditions. Although suitable for children and inexperienced cyclists this is by no means a foolproof track – there are some tight bends and slopes and a fall on the stony surface would be painful, so common sense is required. There are two short road sections, which offer no unusual hazards, but care should be taken on these.

There is an excellent cycle hire centre and shop at Marlow car park offering a range of bikes for hire including tandems. The shop is open all year and can be contacted on 01480 812500.

There are two car parks each on the north and the south sides of the lake. Marlow Park has an exhibition centre and café adjacent to the cycle hire centre. During a peak season visit, the café here could only offer a disappointing selection of less-than-fresh, plastic-encased sandwiches. What a contrast with similar locations in, for example France, where fresh baguettes and crêpes would be the order of the day, and what a waste of a superb location complete with outdoor tables and chairs.

On the south side, the road section passes the Wheatsheaf Pub in Perry which has a good local reputation for food. There is also the Montagu Arms Pub on the opposite side of the lake, a short distance off the route in Grafham.

Cycle hire at Grafham Water

As a base for researching the ride the author camped at the Old Manor Caravan Park in Grafham, this has the advantage of actually being on the ride. Oliver Cromwell once occupied the old white cottage, which is now used as Reception for the camp, and the campgrounds formed part of his garden. Among a full range of amenities the Old Manor Caravan Park offers a solar heated outdoor swimming pool. It comes with a recommendation – for details and bookings telephone 01480 810264.

Getting Started

Starting point – Marlow Park car park. OS Grid Ref. TL 165681

For car travellers Grafham Water is conveniently located three miles from the A1 and A14 junction. Huntingdon Railway Station is five miles away by bike. The National Cycle Network lies far to the north and east and this ride stands some distance from others in the book. **NOTE** – the Marlow Park car park and the other three around the lake are all pay and display.

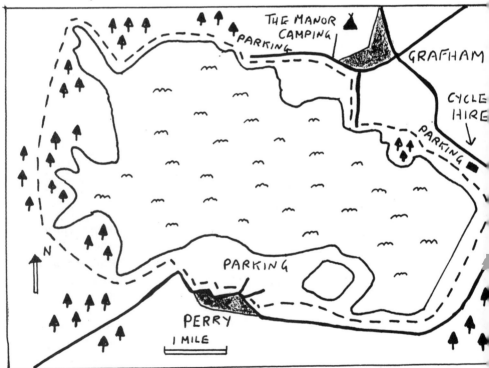

The Route

As the 10-mile ride follows a well-marked cycle path detailed route instructions are not given.

Starting from Marlow Park car park ride anti-clockwise around the lake, first heading east towards the village of Grafham. Remember that the cycle path is shared with walkers and horses and consideration should be shown to all other trail users.

Heading east from Marlow Park, after quarter of a mile the tarmac road through Grafham is reached, passing the Old Manor Caravan Park on the right. Three quarters of a mile after Grafham the tarmac road ends at a car park and the cycle path heads out through the Nature Reserve on the west end of the lake.

A tarmac road then leads into the village of Perry, past the Wheatsheaf Pub on the right. Just after the pub the path separates from the road and leads round the base of the dam that forms the eastern end of the lake, and back to the starting point of the ride in Marlow Park.

Route 17
Fotheringay to Bulwick

Distance: 23 miles

Difficulty Level: 2

Map: OS Landranger 141 – Kettering and Corby; OS
Landranger 142 – Peterborough

Setting the Scene

This is one of the author's favourite rides. On the margins of East Anglia,
located 7 miles west of Peterborough in Northamptonshire, it offers
charming peaceful scenery that contrasts with the flatter open landscapes of the eastern edges of the region. Fortunately most of the traffic
stays on the surrounding "A" roads leaving the minor roads for cyclists to
enjoy. It is particularly pleasing to present a ride of 23 miles that covers
not one inch of "A" or even "B" roads – cycling bliss!

Good cycling and charming scenery is not all that is on offer as the village of Fotheringay, at the start of the ride, is particularly rich in historical
connections. The first castle in Fotheringay can be traced back to 1100,
and has strong (and sad) royal connections. Richard III was born here but
Fotheringay Castle is best known as the place where Mary Queen of
Scots was executed in February 1587 after years of imprisonment. Little
now remains of the castle except some substantial earthworks and a
large piece of fallen masonry down by the river.

Fortunately, the church of St Mary and All Saints still stands in good (if
not complete) repair, and is one of the glories of the area. The church
dates from the 15th century and in common with Wymondham Abbey (see
Route 2) was at one time two churches in one. The parish church still
stands, but attached to it was a (now disappeared) collegiate church for a
college of secular priests. The magnificent west tower dominates the village and surrounding area and the interior is well worth visiting for the
beautiful oak pulpit and heraldic glass.

There are other unspoilt villages on·the ride with their stone houses striking a pleasing contrast to the more typical East Anglian building materials found on other rides. There are pubs, pretty scenery and good riding, which combine to make this one of the most appealing rides in the book.

What to Expect

23 miles without using any "A" or "B" roads makes for very enjoyable cycling. The difficulty level of 2 is derived solely from the length of the ride, if it had been half the length, a comfortable '1' (easiest) would have been awarded.

All the roads have excellent surfaces and are quite suitable for all types of bikes.

There are several pubs and shops on the route, offering good opportunities for lunch and refreshment breaks.

Getting Started

Starting Point: Fotheringay village – OS Grid Ref. TF 933059.

The ride starts from Fotheringay village where there is on-road parking, please show consideration for local residents.

For rail travellers the nearest station is Peterborough 10 miles away.

The ride is on the margins of the region and some way from other features routes. Rutland Water (Route 14) and Grafham Water (Route 16) are the most accessible, each approximately 15 miles away.

The National Cycle Network is some way to the northeast, although not totally inaccessible. The nearest point at Wisbech is some 40 miles away.

The Route

Take the turn **(1)** almost immediately opposite the beautiful parish church signposted to Nassington, Yarwell and Wansford. The village of Wansford, which is 4 miles away, is your next destination.

After 2 miles riding you come to Nassington with the tempting Black Horse Inn on the left and Queens Head Hotel on the right (why two inns in such a tiny village?) plus a village shop.

Yarwell is another mile further on, ride straight through towards Wansford. The road then drops down through a pleasant wooded section to bring you to a T-junction in Wansford. Go left here **(2)** in the direction of Kings Cliffe. After a quarter of a mile take the left turn signposted to Kings

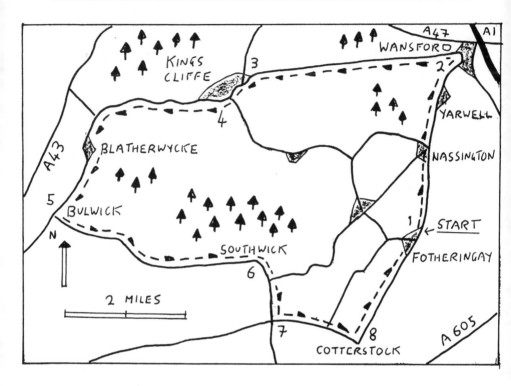

Cliffe which is now 4 miles away. Keep straight ahead on this road, for the final section it crosses the Old Kings Cliffe Airfield with a memorial on the left to the allied airmen of various nationalities who were lost in action in sorties from this airfield.

A straight, fast downhill drops you off the plateau to a T-junction **(3)** go left here in the direction of Kings Cliffe, Apethorpe and Blatherwycke. Cycle straight ahead into Kings Cliffe village centre ignoring the right turn to Blatherwycke. You pass the village store on your left and come to the crossroads in the centre of this pretty village with the parish church of All Saints and St James opposite.

Turn right here **(4)** in the direction of Blatherwycke and Bulwick and ride out of the village, turning left at the T-junction on the edge. Cycle 4 miles to Blatherwycke along this quiet and pretty road which follows Willow Brook all the way to Bulwick.

First you ride through Blatherwycke with its pretty bridge across the Brook. After another mile you reach Bulwick. Go left **(5)** at the T-junction in the centre signposted to Deene, Corby, Kettering and (oddly) A43. Don't panic, this is not even a "B" road – the main road is some way off.

After a couple of hundred yards, take the left turn signposted to Southwick and Oundle. A good, straight, open ride of 4 miles brings you to the village of Shuckburgh with the Shuckburgh Arms Freehouse on the right making a convenient stopping place for lunch.

Just after the pub, turn right **(6)** in the direction of Glapthorn and Oundle. This road takes you uphill to a Water Tower, from which the road dives downhill into Glapthorn **(7)**. At the bottom of the hill turn left towards Cotterstock before you enter the village and ride towards Cotterstock. At the crossroads go straight across again signposted to Cotterstock and Tansor.

Ride through the village of Cotterstock and continue towards Tansor. After crossing the pretty stream with its mill take the left turn **(8)** in the direction of Tansor and Fotheringay.

As you ride into the village of Tansor follow the road as it bears left in the direction of Fotheringay which is now 1¼ miles away. The road passes the impressive Manor House in the village on the right, and leaves Tansor heading out towards Fotheringay with the church now visible dead ahead.

After another mile you cross the bridge spanning the River Nene and return to Fotheringay, the starting point of the ride. The Falcon Pub in Fotheringay offers an excellent opportunity for an end of ride drink!

Routes 18, 19 & 20
Three Rides around Sudbury

Distances: 23 miles; 21 miles; 29 miles

Difficulty Level: 3

Maps: OS Landranger 155 – Sudbury and Stowmarket; OS Landranger 168 – Colchester

Setting the Scene

The three rides presented here are grouped around the biggest of the Suffolk "wool towns" Sudbury. This area is best known for its artists, often-painted landscapes and timber-framed buildings. Sudbury was the birthplace of Thomas Gainsborough, best known for his portraits of 18th century high society. Today it is a bustling commercial centre that has avoided the "Disneyfication" see in some of the other towns in the area. It does have three fine churches, interesting 15th century houses and some worthwhile riverside walks.

The first ride passes through Lavenham, an almost perfectly preserved wool town best know for its Tudor timber framed buildings and 15th century church of St Mary's and Guildhall. Also on this first ride is Kersey, arguably one of the prettiest villages in East Anglia with its steep High Street with a ford at the bottom and church at the top.

The second ride is an altogether more austere affair, exploring the higher ground to the west of Sudbury and south of the River Stour. The ride passes within striking distance of Clare with its overgrown castle keep and massive church. Further on the church of Stoke by Clare has one of the most beautiful pulpits in England dating from the 15th century. This second ride, however, follows the margins of the higher ground, which are devoid of the more picturesque villages found to the east.

This ride offers jolly good riding and some taxing hills. The area is far removed from the billiard table flat Fens of the north of the region. Here the rolling country means the cyclist re-discovers what gears are for, and may start to tax muscles conditioned by the flatter areas of Norfolk and Cambridgeshire.

Routes 18 and 20 are linked by Constable country. John Constable was indisputably one of the few great English artists. He started his schooling in Lavenham before moving to the Grammar School in Dedham, the starting point of the third ride, where his discovery by an amateur artist and collector sent him to London and launched him on his career.

Route 20 is a 29-mile tour of the Stour Valley, visiting several picturesque villages including Stoke-by-Nayland, the subject of a Constable painting hanging in the British Museum. This ride is through classic Constable country, perhaps a little "Disneyland" in its manicured presentation for some tastes, and certainly busy in the summer months.

Route 20 follows the Hull to Harwich cycle route for a short distance, linking these rides to many others in this book. This southerly area of East Anglia should certainly not be missed with its rolling landscape contrasting with the better know areas of the Broads and Fens. The wealth of picturesque villages and links with famous artists combine to make the rides memorable, if more challenging than some of the others in this book.

What to Expect

These rides have more hills than many others in the book so a reasonably level of fitness and a good range of gears is required.

Routes 18 and 20 pass through tourist centres such as Lavenham and Dedham, which are likely to be busy with traffic in the summer months. By contrast Route 19 is largely off the beaten track despite starting from the outskirts of Sudbury and should be quiet virtually all year round.

All the routes use good metalled roads, although some short sections of the third ride, in particular, may be troublesome for lightweight racing wheels.

Both the first and the third Routes offer a good selection of pubs and refreshment breaks en-route. The second ride does not have a single pub, café or shop on its 23-mile length, so self-sufficiency is required here.

To research these rides the author stayed at the excellent Willowmere Caravan and Camping Park in Bures Road, Sudbury. Phone 01787 375559 for details and reservations.

Getting Started

Starting Points

Route 18 – Grotton Wood Nature Reserve Car Park – OS Grid Ref. TL975429

Route 19 – Rodbridge Picnic Site – OS Grid Ref. TL856435

Route 20 – Dedham Car Park – OS Grid Ref. TM058332

Sudbury Railway Station is the end of the line from Colchester. Alternatively the main line to Colchester Station can be used and the National Cycle Network north to Dedham on Route 18 can be followed. The National Cycle Network is used for part of Route 20 and provides a cycling link to many of the other rides in the book. Sudbury is easily accessible by car via the A131 and A134.

Route 18

The ride starts from the car parking area adjacent to Groton Wood Nature Reserve **(1)**. From the car park, turn right out on to the road (west) in the direction of Sudbury.

Keep straight ahead on the road in the direction of Groton, Edwardstone and Sudbury as it bears right ignoring the left turn to Groton but then almost immediately take the left turn marked Byroad **(2)**. This leads to a T-junction, go left here in the direction of Edwardstone and Sudbury. This road drops down to a crossroads, go straight across signposted to Edwardstone.

Continue straight ahead on this road towards Edwardstone taking the right turn after a quarter of a mile signposted to Edwardstone and Brent Eleigh **(3)**. This road takes you past the White Horse Inn, which is tempting for a very early refreshment break, if it is open. Your destination is now Great Wardingfield, four miles beyond the White Horse Inn.

At the next T-junction turn right in the direction of Wardingfield then at the following junction turn left signposted to Sudbury and Long Melford and keep ahead picking up the signs for Great Wardingfield and Lavenham.

There then follows a hilly section, which leads into Great Wardingfield to a T-junction with the B1071 **(4)**. Go right in the direction of Lavenham and Bildeston and after a couple of hundred yards on the "B" road, take the left turn into Ten Tree Road with signposts to Acton and Melford.

After a mile Acton is reached with a well-stocked Village Store on the right. Just after this Store turn right into Barrow Hill signposted to Lavenham **(5)**. After a mile and a half take the left turn signposted to Lavenham **(6)**, shortly after turn right at the next T-junction again in the direction of Lavenham.

This road brings you to a T-junction with the Sudbury Road (by the Peugeot Garage) turn left towards Lavenham and Bury St Edmunds. Ride into Lavenham past the parish church of St Peter and Paul on the left with the Cock Public House on the right offering a mid-ride lunch break. There are public toilets in the car park just beyond the Pub.

In the centre of Lavenham turn right **(7)** into Water Street with the Swan Hotel with its very fine Elizabethan timber framing on the left. Continue down Water Street, with more marvellous timber framed buildings on either side, and at the bottom turn left into a side road marked "local traffic only".

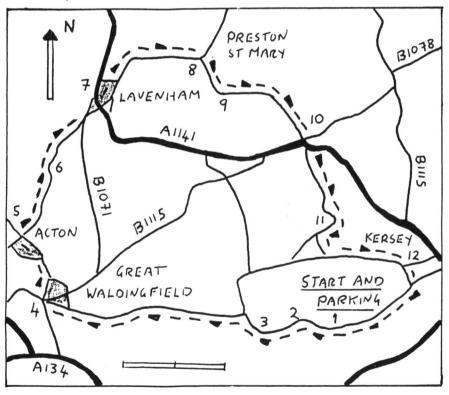

Follow Lower Road as it skirts round the back of Lavenham past the Mill and over the stream to reach a T-junction with a main road. Turn right here signposted to Preston and Brettenham.

After a mile and a half of uninterrupted riding you pass Priory Farm with its barns on the left. Just after the farm take the right turn **(8)** off the main road signposted to Hitcham, Kettlebaston and Brent Eleigh. This road takes you into the village of Preston St Mary with the church of St Mary on the left followed by the picturesque Preston Hall. The road then drops downhill and at the bottom turn left signposted to Monks Eleigh and Bilderstone **(9)**.

After half a mile take the road as it turns right signposted to Monks Eleigh and Bilderstone. After a mile and a half the road comes to a T-junction with the A1141. **(10)** Turn left out on to the A1141 signposted to Hadleigh. Ride past the Corn Craft Shop and tearoom on the left, then almost immediately take the right turn off the "A" road signposted to Lindsey and Boxford.

There is a good ride for a mile and a half through open agricultural areas with big fields of crops. This is quite a high road and can be windy. The road then drops down into the village of Lindsey Tye with a Pub on the left offering a refreshment stop.

In Lindsey Tye at the T-junction **(11)** go right signposted to Groton, Edwardstone and Kersey. After a mile the village of Lindsey is reached, take the left turn opposite the red telephone box into Church Road with the church of St Peter on the left. Ride past the church down this lane with signposts to Kersey and Hadleigh. A downhill section brings you to a T-junction, go left here. After a mile this road drops down to a T-junction in the village of Kersey **(12)**. Go right into the village and down the sloping main street with the Bell Free House on the right to the picturesque ford overlooked by the church.

Ride up the steep hill away from the ford past the church on the right. Keep riding to the T-junction at the top of the hill and turn right signposted to Boxford.

Ride along for half a mile past Sampson's Hall and then take the right turn signposted to Edwardstone. After a mile this road brings you back to the car park at Groton Wood which was the start of the ride.

Route 19

From Rodbridge Picnic Site **(1)** turn left out onto the B1064 in the direction of Fox Earth, crossing a very pleasant section of the River Stour.

After a couple of hundred yards, turn right off the "B" road in the direction of Liston, passing the church of St Catherine on the right, with its distinctive brick built tower contrasting with the flint used in the rest of the building.

There are now two miles of good, uninterrupted riding as the road climbs away from the Stour in the direction of Glemsford. A good climb is followed by a fast downhill, which brings you to a T-junction. Go left at this T-junction **(2)** signposted to Fox Earth with another climb bringing you to a T-junction with the B1074.

(3) Turn right here out onto the "B" road, then after half a mile take the left turn signposted to Pentlow and Belchamps. Stay on this road for two miles as it follows signs to Belchamps and Great Yeldon taking you across rolling countryside disturbed by only the occasional car.

At the next T-junction **(4)** go right in the direction of Clare as the road

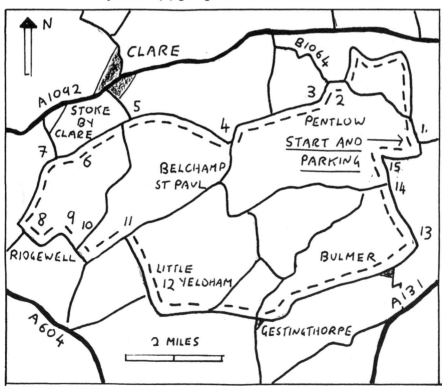

climbs to give sweeping views all round before dropping through Hickford Hill towards the village of Clare and a T-junction.

The route goes left here **(5)** towards Ashen and Ridgewell. However, a diversion to the right takes you into Clare (and to the A1092) to visit the church and remains of the Castle.

Back on the route after turning left at the T-junction, the road crosses more rolling country before dropping downhill steeply to another T-junction **(6)**, turn right here in the direction of Stoke.

At the next T-junction go left **(7)**, noting that you have now entered Essex. A substantial hill leads to another T-junction, go right here in the direction of Ridgewell.

After a mile, just after passing the distinctive weatherboard-clad Bowles Farm on the right, turn left **(8)** in the direction of Tilbury and Juxta Clare. After another mile **(9)** in the hamlet of Tilbury Green take the left turn at the junction again signposted to Tilbury and Juxta Clare.

This road takes you out again through open fields to bring you to another T-junction, turn right towards Great Yeldham. This strangely straight and wide concrete road in the middle of nowhere is a remnant of yet another of East Anglia's military air bases.

At the end of the old taxiway the road narrows and drops down off the plateau into Tilbury Juxta Clare. At the T-junction **(10)** at the bottom of the downhill turn right in the direction of Great Yeldham.

After a quarter of a mile go left at the next T-junction towards Belchamp St Paul. The road climbs gently towards a radio mast. As the road levels turn right into Marshey Road in the direction signposted to Little Yelding and Gestingthorpe **(11)**.

(For those unable to complete the ride without lubrication a detour to the excellent Cherry tree Inn in Belchamp St Paul is available by ignoring the right turn and continuing straight along the road. The Cherry Tree Inn is a Grade 2 listed building with outdoor seating and is a worthwhile detour. The route can be rejoined by cycling from the Inn to Belchamp Otter and then on to Gestingthorpe.)

Back on the main road after turning right ride downhill into Little Yelding with the distinctive wooden bell tower of St John the Baptist on the left. Turn left **(12)** here towards North End, Gestingthorpe and Belchamp Water.

The road then passes the bizarrely named Stone and Faggot Public House. Alas the customers seem to have voted with their feet about the choice of name as at the time of researching the pub appeared to be permanently closed.

The road then continues straight through Guestingthorpe in the direction of Sudbury, before an exciting downhill takes you towards Bulmer. The price is another steep climb into the village, where again the village's pub has closed its doors to thirsty cyclists for the last time to be converted into a house.

Ride along the Sudbury Road and take the left turn into Finch Hill (13). There is no signpost at this junction but Finch Hill is marked with a sign saying "Weight Limit 10 Tons ¾ mile ahead". This road provides a great downhill to a bridge over Belchamp Brook. Immediately after the bridge turn right off this road (14) to climb away from the Brook in a climb that seems especially tiring towards the end of this ride.

At the top of the climb turn right at the T-junction (15) towards Fox Earth. Ride through this pretty village with its pond and church on the left. Follow the road as it drops in a fast downhill to bring you back to a T-junction with the B1074.

Turn right at this T-junction which takes you back across the River Stour to the starting point of the ride in the car park on the right.

Route 20

From the starting point in the free car park (1) in the middle of Dedham turn right out of the car park onto the B1029 and cycle up towards the A12.

Before reaching the A12 take the left turn (2) signposted to Ipswich B1029, Stratford St Mary, Hingham and Flatford, with the church of St Mary, Stratford on the left.

Immediately after passing under the very busy A12 take the right turn in the direction of Hingham. This road brings you to a crossroads, go straight on towards Hingham. As you enter the village of Hingham, bear right at the Green and turn out right (3) onto the B1068 in the direction of East Bergholt and Ipswich.

Almost immediately turn left off the "B" road into an unsignposted turning alongside Yew Tree House. Ride through the village of Raydon in the direction signposted to Shelly and Hadleigh.

As you leave Raydon turn left (4) into the side turning signposted to Shelley. Then immediately after passing the church in Shelley, which is partially hidden behind a hedge, turn left in the direction signposted to Polstead and Stoke by Nayland.

A good climb up this quiet country lane takes you away from the hustle and bustle of the tourist routes. At the top of the climb go left at the T-junction towards Polstead and Stoke, then after a quarter of a mile turn right towards Polstead and cycle for another mile and a half into Polstead with the Cock Public House overlooking the Village Green.

From here ride in the direction of Stoke by Nayland and Boxford down a steep descent to reach a T-junction **(5)**. Go left here towards Stoke by Nayland and Colchester and follow the road through towards Stoke.

After another steep climb away from the River Box take the right at the T-junction with the B1068 **(6)** in the direction of Newton and Sudbury. After a couple of hundred yards on the "B" road take the second turning on the left just after the sharp right-hand bend into Butt road.

This spectacularly narrow lane (with very variable surface, so treat with care) is scarcely wide enough for one car. At the unsignposted T-junction turn left and enjoy the superb riding on these very quiet and narrow back lanes with their interesting hills.

After a mile Gravel Hill drops you down a steep downhill to a T-junction in the centre of Nayland **(7)**. Turn right at the T-junction then right again almost immediately into the main road called Bere Street. Follow this road through Nayland and out to the A134.

With great care cross the "A" road **(8)** diagonally to the right into Whiston Road, which is signposted to Wissington and Burres. Follow this road towards Burres as it runs parallel to the River Stour with good views across on the left.

After 3 miles a crossroads is reached, turn left **(9)** here towards Wormingford. The road passes Smallbridge Hall and crosses the river before reaching Wormingford with the parish church of St Andrew on the right.

You then come to a T-junction in the village with the B1508. Turn left **(10)** out onto the "B" road in the direction of Colchester. After a quarter of a mile take the left turn off the B1508 signposted to Little Horkesley at the point where the main road turns sharp right.

Stay on this road for a mile and a half to reach the crossroads in the middle of Little Horkesley with the Beehive Pub on the left offering an opportunity for a refreshment break.

Go straight on at the crossroads in the direction of Colchester. This road is called Fish Ponds Hill and it drops down then climbs steeply to a junction at the top. Go right here **(11)** in the direction of West Bergholt. After a quarter of a mile turn left into an unsignposted lane which takes you

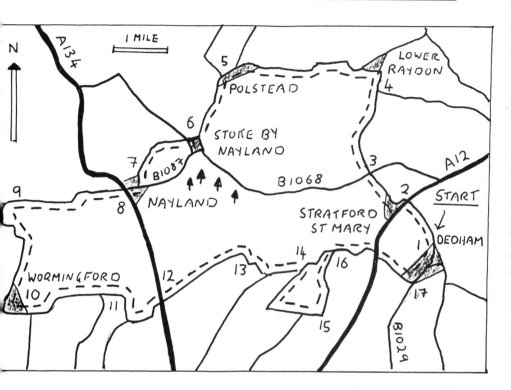

past a reservoir and pumping station on the right. The road then passes through apple orchards and winds back to the A134.

Go straight across the A134 **(12)** into Boxted Church Road and ride straight ahead for a mile and a half towards Boxted. Here are views right across the Stour Valley with the villages on the north side that you rode through earlier clearly visible.

As you ride into Boxted keep riding straight ahead in the direction of Boxted Cross. A steep downhill drops you to a T-junction **(13)**, turn left into Cooks Hill signposted to Dedham. What goes down must come back up again, and another steep climb brings you into Boxted Cross and to another T-junction. Go left here in the direction of Dedham.

After half a mile **(14)** take the first turning off on the right signposted to Langham into Veaudville Road. This road climbs and dives through some very pretty woods, which in springtime are carpeted with bluebells. As you emerge from these woods take the first turning left which is not sign-posted but has a triangle of grass at the junction.

After a quarter of a mile this road brings you into Langham, with the Shepherd and Dog Pub on the right offering the opportunity of a break for refreshments. Ride across the crossroads in the centre of Langham in the direction signposted to Ardleigh. Then ride past Langham Primary School to reach the T-junction at the end of the village.

Turn left here into Wick Road **(15)**, joining the National Cycle Network as it heads north from Colchester towards Norwich. Another steep climb takes you to a crossroads **(16)**, turn right here in the direction of Dedham. After passing Langham Hall with its church on the left, you turn left in the direction of Ipswich and Stratford St Mary, following the National Cycle Network sign.

This main road drops you steeply downhill. Part way down take the right turn signposted into Dedham, taking care at this tricky junction. This right turn takes you on a bridge over the A12, then after a half a mile, with superb views on the left, you reach a T-junction with the B1029. Turn left at this T-junction **(17)** and follow the "B" road back into Dedham.

A left turn into Mill Lane in the centre of Dedham brings you back to the car park and the starting point of the ride.

The River Kennett at Moulton(Route 21)

Route 21
Newmarket Cycleway

Distance: 34 miles

Difficulty Level: 3/4

Map: OS Landranger 154 – Cambridge and Newmarket

Setting the Scene

Newmarket is known world-wide for its stables and horse racing connections. This 34-mile circuit around the town never lets you forget for more than a brief moment that transport in this affluent area is dominated by the four-legged and four-wheeled (BMWs and Range Rovers are commodities in this area, Bentleys and Ferraris are a little less commonplace).

This quite long and sometimes heavily trafficked route is certainly worth riding. However, as this book is an unashamedly personal view, rather than an independent guide, I have to say that this is very different riding to, say, the routes around Fotheringay (Route 17) and Foulsham (Route 4).

One problem is that this is not typical East Anglia (is there any such thing as typical East Anglia in between the extremes of the Fenlands and the Stour Valley?). Newmarket is really one of the gateways to the region, and is set amidst untypical rolling chalk downs. Traffic is a problem; roads dominate the area with the busy A14 trunk road scarcely bypassing the town to the north before joining the main A12 route to Norwich. These trunk roads feed traffic onto the surrounding minor roads, which carry cars whose price ticket and performance sometimes exceed their drivers' capabilities. I met one cyclist on this ride who described it as cycling heaven compared to London where he lived – so it may be, but other routes in this book offer more relaxing riding.

The excellent "Companion Guide to East Anglia" (ISBN 1900639025) hits the nail on the head when it describes the village of Moulton as "Surrey-like". This is Home Counties moved to East Anglia, instead of open fields and skyscapes there are security fences, electric gates and guard dogs. The most extraordinary example of this is found on the road linking

Moulton to Newmarket. Here is situated Warren Place, an incongruous modern private house built recently for Middle Eastern owners at a reputed cost of £10 million and looking for all the world like a cross between a Holiday Inn and a nuclear bunker. Compare this with Guestwick Post Office on Route 4 located inside an old railway cattle truck!

Although not the most peaceful or picturesque ride there is much to interest and stimulate en-route. The villages north-west of Newmarket are less subordinate to the equine economy, the "Companion Guide" acidly explains that the village of Reach is unspoilt "through not being quite beautiful enough for Cambridge commuters to want to come and live there". For its failings this ride will reward the efforts of the more experienced cyclist.

What to Expect

Due to its length, the relatively high traffic volumes, unavoidable and lengthy riding on "B" roads and several busy "A" road crossings, this route is rather a split 3 to 4 rating (4 being the most difficult in the Book).

Compounding the rating is the fact that the ride is really only suitable for mountain bikers as it uses a short 1½-mile section of bridlepath that varies between very muddy in winter and very rutted in summer. Increasing the problem was the fact that at the time of writing this bridle-path was home to several encampments of, what are these days charitably called Travellers, so broken glass, scrap metal and ugly dogs also enlivened the ride. Hopefully by the time of publication, these temporary residents may have travelled on.

This section of bridlepath between Exning and Burwell can be avoided by simply taking the rather busy B1103 between the two villages. Given good weather and an absence of temporary residents the bridlepath should, however, make a more pleasant traffic-free alternative.

Sections of the ride are marked on the 1997 Landranger Map as "Newmarket Cycle Way" although no signs or other evidence of this route appear on the ground. The author tracked down a 1979 local council map of the cycle way but this understandably proved to be less than helpful as it predates the building of the A14 trunk road.

There are plenty of pubs and shops on the route as the ride never crosses open country for more than short distances. Newmarket offers a full range of shops including several cycle outlets.

Getting Started

Starting point: Devils Dyke Nature Reserve car park – OS Grid Ref. TL 581649.

For rail travellers, two stations are located on the route at Dullingham and Kennet. For cycle tourists this ride is located well to the west of the National Cycle Network, although Route 19 can be accessed by a linking ride of 13 miles from Clare to Cheveley.

The Route

From Devil's Dyke Nature Reserve car park **(1)** turn left onto the B1102 and ride along to Swaffham Prior. For the first section the footpath on the far side of the "B" road is an official cycle path. Stay on the B1102 through Swaffham Prior passing the Prior House on your right before reaching Swaffham Bulbeck. Take the first turning on the left **(2)** in Swaffham Bulbeck into Heath Road signposted to Dullingham and Stetchworth. Then turn left again in the direction of "Newmarket 5½ miles". Follow this excellent straight road for 2½ miles across a bridge over the A12 to a crossroads with the A1303. Go carefully straight across the main road towards Dullingham.

After another 1¼ miles a T-junction with the A1304 is reached **(3)**. Go right here, then almost immediately left into the side turning signposted to Dullingham 2½ miles. On the right the Cambridge and Newmarket Polo Club with its carefully manicured lawn sets the tone for much of the ride.

A mile further on, pass over a level crossing with Dullingham Station on the right, then after another half a mile a crossroads with the B1061 with the Kings Head Pub on the left is reached. Go straight across this in the direction of Stetchworth and Woodditton. Ride on for three-quarters of a mile into Stetchworth and turn right **(4)** at the T-junction with the Marquis of Granby Pub on your left in the direction of Woodditton.

After 1½ miles you reach Woodditton with the Black Birds Pub on the left dating from 1642 and offering food and drink. Continue straight through the village and on for another mile to Saxon Street. At the T-junction in Saxon Street **(5)** turn right into The Street towards Cheveley and Kirtling passing the Reindeer Pub on the right. After less than a quarter of a mile take the left turn into Cheveley Road signposted to Cheveley and Ashley. After another quarter of a mile turn left into Oak Lane at Oak Tree Corner in the direction of Cheveley and Morton, passing another pub and a general store.

You then ride through the village of Cheveley with the parish church of St Mary on the right to reach the B1063. Go straight across the "B" road in the direction of Morton and Kenford. You are now in serious racehorse country with two large stud farms on this road. A good, fast, straight road then drops you downhill to a T-junction with Dalham Road.

Turn left here **(6)** towards Chippenham and Isleham and ride into Moulton with a Post Office and Stores on the left. Moulton has two 15thcentury bridges, one of them being a picturesque packhorse design.

Stay on the sometimes-busy B1058 as it leaves Moulton and follow it towards Chippenham, which is 6 miles away. At the crossroads with the busy B1506 go straight across in the direction of Fordham.

The road then crosses the busy A12 on a bridge and comes to a railway bridge with Kennett Station on the left. After another mile you reach a roundabout over the busy A11, go straight on here towards Chippenham and Fordham. On the right is an off-road activity park where you can do everything from driving a tank to racing moto-cross bikes.

After another three-quarters of a mile the grounds of Chippenham Park are reached on the left, behind the brick wall and trees. The road skirts around this large estate which is yet another Stud Farm complete with security patrols. It is difficult to accept that you are in rural East Anglia, this could just as easily be the hinterland of Dallas.

Ride into the centre of Chippenham and opposite the Tharp Arms Pub, which offers a lunch stop; take the left turn **(7)** off the main road towards Snailwell and Newmarket. Ride on for 2 miles into Snailwell. In the centre of Snailwell turn right **(8)** around the triangle of grass in the centre and leave the village along the road called The Street, past the weight limit sign. On the left is the George and Dragon Pub, which offers another opportunity for a lunch break. This road leads you out of Snailwell past a surprisingly large industrial area to a crossroads with the busy A142. Cross the "A" road with care into the road opposite signposted to Landwade and Exning.

Ride on for 2 miles into Exning noting that the area's preoccupation with horses extends to a large and palatial equine hospital on the right. In Exning you come to a T-junction **(9)**, turn right here then immediately right again out onto the B1103 in the direction of Burwell with the White Horse Pub opposite. Take care at this tricky junction where you twice have to turn across on-coming traffic.

After just a couple of hundred yards, as the "B" road bears left carefully turn right into Northend Road, ignoring the cul-de-sac sign. This green

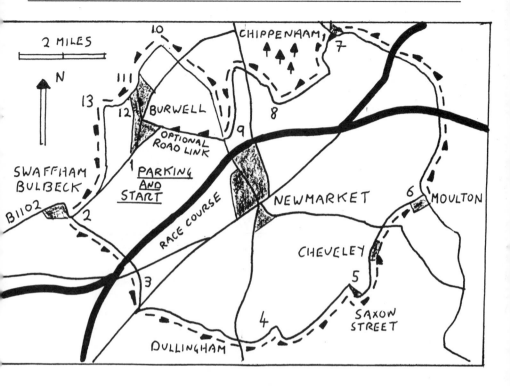

country lane is a quiet contrast to the bustling "B" road that is left behind. The approaching off-road section, which may offer mud, bumps and unfriendly dogs, can be avoided by ignoring this right turn and following the B1103 into Burwell.

Keep straight ahead as the good metalled road suddenly turns into a track and then, after passing a house, becomes a definitely off-road route that will be muddy in bad weather. This section hosted some temporary residents at the time of researching, complete with canine friends.

The bridleway brings you to the B1102, go straight across onto the track opposite which is signposted Public By-way (10). After a quarter of a mile you reach a T-junction with a metalled road, go left and ride down into Burwell where the Anchor pub awaits to soothe nerves if any canines remain resident on the bridlepath.

Ride through Burwell to the Fox Pub on the left. Immediately opposite the pub turn right (11) off the main road into the unsignposted to Hythe Lane. After crossing a stream the road turns sharp left and leaves the village running parallel to a stream towards the village of Reach. After passing a poultry farm you come to a T-junction with a main road. Turn right here **(12)** – there are no signposts.

Ride into the pretty village of Reach. The excellent Kings Head Pub awaits for a celebratory drink as you have covered 32 miles with only 2 miles more to go. **(13)** Turn left and left again opposite the Kings Head to leave the village in the direction of Swaffham Prior. After a mile, the first turning on the left as you enter Swaffham Prior brings you up to the B1102. Turn left here and cycle back along the cycle path to return to the starting point at the Devil's Dyke Nature Reserve car park.

More East Anglia books from Sigma:

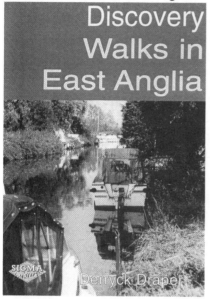

Discovery Walks in East Anglia

Since the 15th century, the wool trade has shaped the architecture and lifestyle of the towns and villages of rural Anglia. From this starting point Derryck Draper has devised 30 discovery walks, each with a heritage theme, giving good coverage of the landscape of East Anglia and considerable insight into the history of the area. His walks range from 4 to 10 miles and suit walkers of all abilities. £6.95

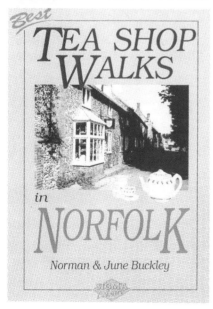

Best Tea Shop Walks in Norfolk

25 gentle walks, suitable for all the family, spread throughout Norfolk's countryside and coastline. Most routes are centred on Norfolk's towns, villages and stately homes, and all feature essential information on the landscape, social and industrial history, and interesting features met along the way. Norman & June Buckley, Britain's - tea shop walk experts - believe that a 'tea shop stop' adds a whole new dimension to country walking - and this new title contains a huge range of establishments - some in out of the way and unusual places. £6.95

Best Tea Shop Walks in Suffolk

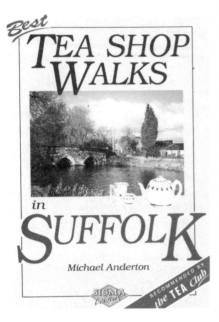

The county of Suffolk is laced with over 3,500 miles of public path, criss-crossing the landscape to provide the walker with unlimited access to places of interest. Walk through a wide diversity of terrain - from the coastal margin of the Heritage Coast, the valleys of the river Stour, Deben and Gipping, to the dry sandy soils of the remote Breckland. And after your walk why not reward yourself with a few home made cakes in the afternoon or a bowl of hot soup and a piece of bread on a cold day? -The book also guides you to a wide range of unique tea shops, often in out of the way places and unusual buildings. £6.95

In case of difficulty, or for a free catalogue, please contact: **SIGMA LEISURE, 1 SOUTH OAK LANE, WILMSLOW, CHESHIRE SK9 6AR.** Phone: 01625-531035; Fax: 01625-536800.

E-mail: sigma.press@zetnet.co.uk . Web site: http//www.sigmapress.co.uk VISA and MASTERCARD orders welcome.